Unshackled & Growing is an extrac[...] Muslim who is seeking to learn mo[...] with comparing the worldviews of Islam and Christianity. Dr. Jabbour's familiarity with Arabic and Islamic culture and the concerns of Muslim people make this an insightful book. As a former Muslim who has come to faith in Jesus, I wish that I had the benefit of this book during my own journey.

ABDU MURRAY
Lawyer and co-founder, Aletheia International

This unique and valuable book explains in simple and straightforward language how curiosity can lead to genuine attraction to the man Jesus and then to personal trust.

COLIN CHAPMAN
Professor and Author

Are you curious to know the truth about Jesus' life and message? Then read this book. There is no other like it. Nabeel Jabbour has written this book to people who admire Jesus' life and wonder if He was more than a prophet. He writes with the historical and biblical accuracy of a scholar and with the gentleness of a true follower of Jesus.

JIM PETERSEN
Teacher and Author

For any person who wants to know more about Jesus Christ, *this book is a must.*

HEND HANNA, MD, MPH
Assistant Professor, M.D. Anderson Cancer Center, Houston, Texas

I want to strongly urge you, my colleagues and my friends who love Muslims, to introduce this book to them.

RICK LOVE
Author and International Director of Frontiers

Numerous books that I read about Christianity failed to help me explain my faith effectively to my Muslim family and friends. Dr. Jabbour's book is readable with stories and illustrations that speak to the Muslim mind. He presents the pure and biblical Gospel and invites the reader to be a "follower of Jesus," not a Western Christian.

DR. HATICE TURKER
University Professor

The issue of who Jesus really is in the Muslim mind has always raised questions and debate. This book gives an excellent explanation about Jesus and the "true *Injil*" with simple language and clear illustrations. Every page is worthwhile reading.

SHARIFAH AINA ZAHARI
Scholar

The Christian life is both coming to Christ through faith in Him and then walking with Him the rest of one's days. Dr. Jabbour addresses both of these issues with clarity and simplicity.

JERRY BRIDGES
Author of the best-seller *The Pursuit of Holiness* and other books

This book summarizes years of ministry via a practical plan and lucid principles that anyone can understand. I heartily commend it.

ABE WIEBE
Former International Director of Arab World Ministries

Dr. Jabbour has lived what he writes about in *Unshackled & Growing*. You can literally smell the gun-smoke of his life on every page. If you are interested in reaching out in Christian love to your Muslim friends and neighbors, *don't miss this book!*

EDWARD J. HOSKINS, MD, PhD
Author of *A Muslim's Heart*

Unshackled & Growing

Muslims and Christians
on the Journey to Freedom

Dr. Nabeel T. Jabbour

dawsonmedia
P.O. Box 6000 • Colorado Springs, CO 80934

A MINISTRY OF ◯ THE NAVIGATORS®

To my friend Samuel in Egypt.
Celebrating our journey together since 1975.

إهــــداء

إلى صديقي العزيز صموئيل

الرفيق على الطريق منذ عام ١٩٧٥

Contents

PART III: THE MANUAL: GROWING IN CHRIST

APPENDICES

FOREWORD

WHEN AN AUTHOR WRITES, HE HAS TO CHOOSE HIS AUDIENCE. NABEEL Jabbour has chosen to address this book to people who are on a quest to know the true meaning of Jesus' life and message. It is written by an Arab to the Muslim mind, yet anyone who is asking questions about Jesus will be richer for the reading. This book is both accurate and comprehensive, yet it remains very readable. That is because Nabeel is one of those rare persons who is both a scholar and a practitioner. He has lived by the things he has written on these pages—and along the way he has effectively taught many others to do the same.

The real test of any book is the effect it has on its chosen audience. As this manuscript was taking shape, Nabeel sent copies to people who are on this quest and asked them for their critique. The following letter is Dr. Fatima Al Makky's response.

Dear Dr. Jabbour,

Words cannot begin to describe the blessings I was covered with during the reading of your book. I really felt the Holy Spirit whispering in my ear "See, Fatima? This is what I mean." Your book came at this time in my life to assure me that we are worshiping a living God, and He will never forsake us. I could hear Him telling me what He said in Jeremiah 40:4, "I free you this day from the chains that were on your hand . . . and I will look after you." He, the almighty God Himself, is looking after me. I love the Arabic translation of this phrase, which says 'aieny 'alaiki *("I am looking after you."). He is not just glancing at me. He is looking after me.*

I remember when I first started being discipled by a Christian woman. I told her: "I can study the four gospels with you, but please not the Old Testament, nor the book of Acts, and most definitely not the Epistles. The Old Testament reminds me of the strict law. The book of Acts doesn't minister to me, and I don't care who went where and did what. As for the Epistles, I do not want to

9

*even go there. These are just letters that are limited to a historical
time and place, and they do not apply to me anyway."*

*The Christian lady was very patient with me and continued to
disciple me, and God used her as a "cable to jump-start our dead
batteries"—our family, who have all become followers of Christ.*

*Months went by and the lady who was discipling me traveled to
another country. I found myself beside my bed one night asking Him,
"Was it a dream? What is next? What am I supposed to do now?
Why are You leaving me in the middle of the ocean when I don't
know how to swim alone?"*

*He answered me through your book, saying: "Fatima, you are
unshackled now. Get up and walk. It's that easy. Follow ME."*

*I confess to you that I had to put the book down so many times
while reading it to catch my breath. I sobbed so many times. I
cried. I laughed. I felt the Lord hugging me and rocking me back
and forth with my head on His chest saying, "Yes, my child. I love
you that much. Do not worry. You will never be alone again. I will
always be here for you."*

*Dr. Jabbour, I went and got my Bible and started reading
the book of Acts again and found a new meaning in the saying,
"That is the rest of My story." I felt the agony of the disciples as
they struggled between reality and doubts. I felt HIM; I could see
His teary eyes looking at me, and hugging me saying: "It is OK,
Fatima. I love you for who you are. You are not a cheater, Fatima.
You still can say* al hamdu lellah *("thanks to God") instead of
saying* noshkor al rab *(Christian terminology for "we thank the
Lord") if you want to. You still can say* besm Allah al rahman al
raheem *("in the name of God the merciful and compassionate")
when you start your car in the morning. It is OK, Fatima. You
are not a cheater. I AM still the same yesterday, today, tomorrow,
and forever. So you still can say* sadaka Allah al azeem *("truly
and with truth God has spoken") after you read the Bible. You do
not have to change your language around Christians. I love you,
Fatima Al Makky, for who you are. If I wanted another copy of the
Christians, I would have created you in a Christian family, but
I want YOU. So relax in my arms, child, and don't kick." Do you
believe it? I slept for a whole two days afterward!*

*Thank you so very much for giving me the honor of reading
what the Lord told you to say to us, the new believers, through His
Holy Spirit. Once again, I am 100 percent sure that God is going*

to use this book. I am basking now in God's love. One day God is going to use me as a cable to jump-start other dead batteries.

Sincerely,

Fatima Al Makky, Ph.D.

As you read on, ask God to meet you, as Fatima did.

Jim Petersen

ACKNOWLEDGMENTS

I AM EXTREMELY GRATEFUL FOR THE INSIGHTS AND CONTRIBUTIONS that a variety of friends have made to this book. I could not have written it without their help. The hours and the effort they have spent reviewing the manuscript are invaluable. You know who you are. I am deeply grateful. I am also grateful to the staff of Dawson Media for making this book a reality.

INTRODUCTION

IN MY FINAL YEAR IN HIGH SCHOOL IN LEBANON, I WAS A POOR STUDENT in mathematics and the sciences. I vividly remember a terrible day when I was in physics class. The teacher was explaining a tough problem, and I did not have a clue about what was being taught. With my eyes wide open, I was staring at the teacher and daydreaming. In my daydream, I imagined myself to be a great and famous scientist, a physicist, respected by the world and, of course, by my teacher and classmates. Then, all of a sudden, the teacher threw a small piece of chalk at me, and with a jolt, I was brought back to my painful reality.

I inherited my religion like most Arab Muslims, Christians, and Jews do. Because my parents were Christians, I grew up as a Christian. A few weeks after that incident in the physics class, I had an encounter with Christ, and since that time I have been going through a process of transformation and growth, of being unshackled from insecurities and hang-ups. I would like to become a spiritual giant in an instant, but that doesn't happen. I continue to struggle at times with my insecurities, and God has been very gracious and patient with me.

My life's journey over the years allowed me to live in Syria during my childhood, then for many years in Lebanon, then in Egypt, and finally in the United States. One of my unique experiences was the privilege of studying by correspondence for a doctorate degree in theology and comparative religions during our years in Egypt. The focus of my study was Islamic Fundamentalism. For years I read many of the writings of Islamic Fundamentalist leaders like Hasan Al-Banna, Sayyid Qutb, and Khumeini. For my doctorate, I was trained not to come to Islam with a prejudiced and already-made-up mind, but to look at Islam, Islamic Fundamentalism, and Muslim fundamentalists as "phenomena." I wanted to learn to stand in the shoes of those Muslims and see the world through their eyes. What an experience! As a result, I learned to love Muslims in a way I had never known before. Another dimension to my uniqueness is my understanding of Christianity and the West. So, over the years, I learned to "interpret" Islam to Western Christians in a way that helps them develop respect and understanding.

I have written this book for people who fall into the following groups:

- Muslims who desire to know Jesus in a new way and want to have an encounter with Him.
- Muslims who have had an encounter with Christ recently and desire to grow steadily in their walk with Him. These people do not want to waste time; they want to seriously pursue God.
- Muslims who have had an encounter with Christ in the past but are living a mediocre life with God. They have had a relationship with Christ for years but have not been faithful. They already know God, yet in some ways they are still shackled. If you belong to this category, determine that you want to be serious in your walk with Christ, and use this book as a fresh start.
- Christians who love Muslims and desire for their Muslim friends to be exposed to Jesus Christ as He is presented in the Bible.
- The mature follower of Christ who wants to disciple a new believer or a group of new believers in their daily walk. I recommend that you read through the book and skim through the manual before you use it to lead others.

All of us, like me in my physics class, daydream. We attempt to escape from our realities by rationalizing our mistakes, playing the victim, or trying to convince ourselves that we are earning the acceptance of God and His mercy through our strenuous religiosity. Once in a while something happens—someone throws chalk at us and we find ourselves being awakened to see our reality and to face the truth squarely. These moments of personal honesty are extremely important. Make the most of these moments, because with time and age our egos and defense mechanisms become more professional, to the degree that these moments of honesty become very brief or may disappear completely.

I do not know why you are reading this book. Regardless of how devout you have been or how far you have gone in your pursuit of God, please determine that you will try to be honest with yourself and God as you read. Take advantage of the brief moments of honesty that might come your way. Let them unshackle you and help you grow.

This book is written to those who want to learn to stand before they learn how to walk and to walk before they learn to run. Walking on the straight road with Jesus the Son of Mary is a process. Getting to know Jesus in a deep way and walking with Him will be the focus of this book. God does not want to frustrate you! Muslims believe that *"No soul shall have a burden laid on it greater than it can bear"* (Al-Baqara: Surah 2 verse 233). God has promised, *"No temptation has seized you except what is common to man. And God is faithful; he will not let you be tempted beyond what you can bear. But when you are tempted, he will also provide a way out so that you can stand up under it"* (1 Corinthians 10:13).

How to Use This Book

This is not an ordinary book. It is not primarily intended to fill you with more information. Instead, it is designed to give you a fresh and accurate perspective on what the Bible says about Jesus Christ and help you put into practice what you are learning. The third part of this book is like an instruction manual. It will help you learn how to read regularly in the Bible—not in a legalistic, routine manner but with joy—and how to find answers to your issues and questions. Please do not continue reading this book until you have determined to come with an *open mind* and are ready to take the steps needed to get unshackled and free from bondage. Are you ready for a great adventure?

If you have already had an encounter with Christ, do not wait until you finish Part I and Part II before you start on Part III. You can go through the book and the manual simultaneously. *If you have not had an encounter with Christ, do not start on the manual yet.* The manual is intended to help you, from the first day after your encounter with Christ, walk steadily with Jesus on the straight road.

Please do not read this book hurriedly. It will be good if you pray before and after you read, asking God to reveal more of Jesus to you. You can read this book on your own or with a small group of one or more others. What is important is that you read with an attitude of looking at the "mirror" of God's Word to find in your own life what sins and defilement need to be abandoned and washed clean, and which shackles need to be broken.

If you are reading this book with others, a weekly meeting (that can take up to 60 or 90 minutes) can take this form:

- Begin with a simple prayer, asking God to reveal Jesus more clearly.
- Read together one chapter or part of a chapter, and discuss it together (30 to 40 minutes). The questions at the end of every chapter will be helpful.
- Using the Bible reading guide in the manual, share what you have read from the Bible during the previous week (20 to 30 minutes).
- Check with one another the verses that you have memorized from the Bible, which are suggested in the manual (5 to 10 minutes).
- Pray about how to put into practice what you have learned.

I am looking forward, my new friend, to journeying with you in this great venture of faith.

PART I

UNSHACKLED

CHAPTER 1

UNWRAPPING

THE GOSPEL

MY DEAR MUSLIM FRIEND, AS WE START ON THIS JOURNEY TOGETHER, I wonder how much you know about the difference between true followers of Christ and "cultural" Christians. Just as there are cultural Muslims, there are also cultural Christians. Cultural Muslims tend to believe that certain parts of the Qur'an are relevant today and other parts were relevant only in the seventh century. Cultural Christians tend to believe certain parts of the Bible but not others. Some of these cultural or nominal Christians are even zealous and fanatical enough to wage religious wars in the name of Christianity. But please do not confuse them with true followers of Christ.

Nor should you confuse members of sects, such as Mormons and Jehovah's Witnesses, with true followers of Christ. Please make these distinctions.

I wonder, when you hear the word "Gospel" (*Injil*), what comes to your mind? To many Muslims, the word "Gospel" means the New Testament—the part of the Bible that tells about Jesus and what happened after His arrival on earth. To others who have had more exposure to Christians, the Gospel may be a formula or dry doctrinal statement. To others, it is a set of texts from the Bible presented in a logical argument leading to a conclusion. To others, it is a condescending message telling you that the only way to enter the kingdom of God is to become a copy of Christians, including our prejudices and bigotry. Please forgive us for communicating this to you. The Gospel is none of the above.

The word "*Injil*," or Gospel, comes from the Greek word "*Angelos*," meaning "good news." When I refer to the Gospel, or *Injil*, in this book, I am always talking about *Angelos*, the Good News of Jesus and what He did for us.

WHAT IS THE GOSPEL?

A few years ago, I spent many hours with my friends, followers of
Christ in the Middle East, studying the topic, "What is the Gospel?" We
wanted to know the *minimum essentials* for a person to enter the kingdom of God. What does it take for someone to get into paradise?

According to the Bible, two thieves were crucified along with Christ
on His right and left sides. One of them was arrogant and defiant; the
other was repentant. The repentant thief asked Jesus to remember him,
and Jesus told him, *"Today you will be with me in paradise"* (Luke 23:43).

This thief on the cross was a great lesson for me. He (1) recognized
who Jesus truly was and (2) responded to Him with faith. He did not
have time to get baptized, read the Bible, or go to church. Yet Jesus
promised him, "Today you will be with me in paradise."

In addition to this passage, our group tried to find answers to our
question by looking through the whole Bible, cover to cover. My conclusion was simple and profound: The Gospel (or the Good News) is:
(1) Jesus Christ, (2) no more, and (3) no less.

At the conclusion of our study time, I went to a room alone and
wrapped a tangerine with a paper. I then taped it and wrote on the
paper, "Change my name from a Muslim name to a Christian name."
Then I wrapped another paper around it and wrote on it, "Abandon my
Muslim family and join Christianity." Then on another paper I wrote, "I
need to be ready to attack Islam," and I continued with another one and
another one. By the time I finished, the tangerine became almost as big
as a volleyball.

Then I went back to the group and showed them the ball of paper,
telling them there was something inside that symbolized the Gospel.
They didn't know what it was. I showed them what I had written on the
outer sheet of paper and asked, "Is this the Gospel?" They said, "No." I
unwrapped the outer sheet and showed them what was written on the
next sheet, asking, "Is this the Gospel?" Again they said, "No." I kept
unwrapping the layers one after another until there was only one wrapping sheet left. By then, they could see that there was a tangerine inside,
and they started laughing. When I got to the last sheet, I asked them, "Is
this the Gospel?" and they shouted, "No!" Finally, I unwrapped the last
sheet, leaving only the tangerine, and asked, "Is this the Gospel?" They
screamed out: "Yes!" I surprised them by saying, "No." Then I peeled the
tangerine, threw the peelings away, and said, "*This* is the Gospel."

Many times when we Christians "present" the Gospel, or Jesus
Christ, to our Muslim brothers and sisters, you do not see Jesus. All you

see is the wrapping we have put on Him. Many times the wrapping is offensive. Imagine a young man bringing an expensive diamond ring to propose to the girl he loves. Now imagine that instead of having the diamond ring placed in a beautiful little box, he has wrapped it in filthy paper. If this ring is packaged so distastefully, will she accept the gift?

HISTORY OF THE WORD "CHRISTIAN"
The term "Christian" has accumulated 20 centuries of meaning. It may surprise you to know, however, that it appeared only three times in the New Testament 2,000 years ago. Let's take a look at how the word was used then.

In the book of Acts, which details the lives of the earliest believers in Christ shortly after His death, we read: *"For a whole year Barnabas and Saul met with the church and taught great numbers of people. The disciples were called Christians first at Antioch"* (Acts 11:26–27). The believers in Antioch were so excited about Jesus that He became their purpose for living. In the United States, people who loved President Reagan very much were called Reaganites. In Antioch, people who loved Christ very much were referred to as "Christians."

The word is used a second time in Acts 26:28: *"Then Agrippa said to Paul, 'Do you think that in such a short time you can persuade me to be a Christian?'"* In this second instance, King Agrippa, who was interrogating the apostle Paul, used the word in an exclamatory manner. He was telling Paul: "Do you think that in such a short time you can convince me to become crazy about Jesus?"

In the third and final instance, we see that to be a Christian was to belong to a persecuted minority: *"If you suffer, it should not be as a murderer or thief or any other kind of criminal, or even as a meddler. However, if you suffer as a Christian, do not be ashamed, but praise God that you bear that name"* (1 Peter 4:15–16). Christians paid a high cost as they suffered for their beliefs.

Over 20 centuries, the word "Christianity" has accumulated many layers and means something very different than it did initially. Allow me, my Muslim friend, to share with you briefly about our Christian history, including some of the things Christians are ashamed of.

According to the book *Christian Jihad*, from A.D. 30 to A.D. 324, Christians were a persecuted minority. But then a courtship between the state and the church began, and the church submitted to the state. From A.D. 325 to A.D. 1000, the church and the state cooperated as partners, and the relationship between the two appeared to be harmless.

325-1000 AD

The Christians were protected by the state, and the church related to the state in an "unholy matrimony." From A.D. 1000 to A.D. 1300, the church became political and very powerful. During this period the Crusades and the Inquisition took place. The church dedicated itself to the destruction of "splinter groups" of Christians who had divorced themselves from the "real church." During this stage, the church became a "mistress" to the state. The period that followed led to the Reformation and the Enlightenment.

Before the conversion of Constantine the persecutors of Christians were almost always Roman pagans who wanted to . . . eliminate the ever expanding "cult" of Christianity. . . . At the time of Nero (54–68 AD), Decius (249–251 AD) and Diocletian (284–305 AD) . . . Christians were being thrown to the lions, hung as living candles, or decapitated. With Constantine (312–337 AD) Christianity was recognized as an authentic religion. Once feared and persecuted, Christianity now became favored and pampered. . . . The emperor, once the fiercest enemy of Christianity, became its greatest supporter and promoter. . . . Christian bishops now accompanied Constantine to war, praying for his success and guarding his soul. . . . With time the persecuted became the persecutor. . . . Many of them took joy in the fact that Constantine was enthusiastically endorsing Christianity while demolishing pagan religions. The power of God shifted from the church to the state. . . . The Crusades were waged against the Muslims and Jews and lasted for a long time (1095–1291 AD). In his short sightedness Pope Urban II was obsessed with power. He promised that whoever lifted arms against the Muslims entered into a holy war and would be saved. Either by shedding the blood of the infidels, or by dying on the battlefield, the warrior was promised eternal salvation. Pope Urban II did not foresee the potential dangers of success. The recapture of Jerusalem brought more difficulty. The means by which the Crusades were victorious breached all boundaries of Christian ethics. It was their brutality that became legend.[1]

The story goes on and on until today when Christianity is surrounded by layers of different meanings. These layers include politics and

---

1 Ergun Mehmet Caner and Emir Fethi Caner, *Christian Jihad* (Grand Rapids: Kregal Publications, 2004), 118–119, 157–161.

economics, as well as social, religious, and psychological factors.

Please forgive us for the evil that has been committed in the name of Christianity. Please allow yourself to differentiate between Jesus and the layers that have been wrapped around Him through the centuries.

THE WRAPPINGS

Are you familiar with the saying, "Don't throw the baby out with the bathwater"? I was reminded of this expression one day as I talked with an atheist who was furious with evangelical Christians, bashing them with his talk. Most probably his favorite bumper sticker was: "God, save me from Your followers."

We talked about the old days when mothers washed their babies in small metal tubs. After the baby was clean, the mother took the baby out of the dirty water and then disposed of the dirty water. With no indoor plumbing, the mother likely threw the water outside. I turned to my atheist friend and apologized for the dirty water in Christian history and in my own personal history. Then I asked him the question: "How did Jesus offend you?" He responded, "He did not offend me at all." So I told him: "Don't throw the baby out with the bathwater."

My friend, can you distinguish between Christ and the wrappings? The wrappings could include misconceptions on your part and things that we Christians, consciously or unconsciously, communicate. What do you hear us say to you? What are your fears? Do you have misconceptions?

As you consider the list below, ask yourself, "What is the Gospel, and what are the wrappings?" Maybe there are things on this list you thought you had to do to become a follower of Jesus. But how many of these are true requirements, and how many are misconceptions?

To become a follower of Christ, I must:

- Change my name from Muhammad to a Christian name like Steve or Peter.
- Believe that God had sex with Mary, and Jesus is their son. (For more on this, see Chapter 2.)
- Not dare share my doubts about certain Bible passages with my close Christian friends so that I will not offend them.
- Get baptized very soon and tell everybody about it, especially my family, or else Christians will be suspicious of my faith.
- Not kneel like Muslims do when they pray but talk with God while sitting down on a chair or on a pew speaking to His Majesty. I should learn to relax and to pray even while putting one leg over the other.

- Start attacking Islam, Muhammad, and the Qur'an to prove to my-self that my total exodus from Islam is complete and, therefore, my belonging to Christianity is real. The more I attack Islam, the more Christians will truly believe that I have become one of them.
- If I am a woman, hang a golden cross around my neck, wear short skirts and sleeveless dresses, and stop wearing *hijab* (a Muslim woman's head dress) so that I show my Muslim family I am no more like them.
- Drink all the alcohol and eat all the pork I want because I am free.
- Live without restraint and do anything I want because my sins are all forgiven.
- Be careful not to have slips of the tongue by using Muslim termi-nology such as: *Al hamdulilah* ("Thanks to God"), *Insha Allah* ("If God wills"), *Asalamu 'alaykum* ("Peace on you"), *Bismilah* ("In the name of God"), and *Bismilah rahman rahim* ("In the name of God the merciful and the compassionate").
- See Arabs and Muslims as the enemy, calling their God a demon and their prophet Muhammad a terrorist and a demon-possessed pedophile.
- Work hard on a legalistic "checklist" that includes reading the Bi-ble every day, memorizing verses from the Bible, going to church, learning to sing Christian songs, and getting very busy in church activities. It will be a heavy burden, but this is what is required.
- If I live in America, I should become a Republican and start listen-ing to radio talk shows that support capitalism and democracy. I should attempt to become as Westernized as I can.

As you look at this list, what is the Gospel and what are the wrap-pings? If the Gospel truly is Jesus Christ—no more, no less—then *everything on this list* is merely wrapping or misconception.

The follower of Christ *does* need to read, study, and meditate on the Bible for survival and growth, but not in a legalistic manner (i.e., trying to appease God and earn His acceptance through vigorous religiosity). It can be done in an atmosphere of God's acceptance and favor.

As you continue reading this book, you will come to understand more and more what it means to live in an atmosphere of grace. Grace is unmerited and undeserved favor. It means experiencing God's love even though we are not worthy of it. Grace does not mean that God re-laxes His standards and accepts us as we are. Rather, it is God's blessings through Christ to us who deserve His wrath and curse.

As you continue reading, I do hope that you will shift your focus from the "dirty bathwater" to the "baby." Do not let your misconceptions keep you from learning more about Jesus and His purpose for coming to earth.

Reflection and Discussion Questions

1. Have you been offended by Christians who imposed the "wrappings" of the Gospel on you? What have been some of your painful experiences with Christians in the past?
2. Are there similarities between our Christian history and your Muslim history?
3. Are there parts of your Muslim history that you are proud of and parts that you wish were different?
4. Please consider carefully every point on the list on pages 25 and 26. What is wrong with every point on this list?
5. Where is the Gospel, and where are the wrappings in the points on the list?
6. What are your misconceptions about Christ? What will it take to correct these misconceptions?

NoTEWoRTHY:

• Followers of Jesus   vs. "cultural" Christians (p21)

p21 • Gospel = (1) Jesus Christ, (2) no more, (3) no less

p22 • Christians often present "Jesus with wrappings" rather than biblical Jesus

p25 • Apologize for "dirty water" in Christian & personal history. Ask question, "How did Jesus offend you?"

CHAPTER 2

GOD'S ONENESS

AND THE VISIT

TO OUR PLANET

THE IDEA THAT GOD IS ONE IS CENTRAL IN ISLAM. IT MIGHT SURPRISE
you that the Bible also teaches that God is one. In the Bible, we see
complexity in the being of God, yet at the same time there is oneness.
Some Muslims think that the "Trinity" Christians talk about is made up
of God, Mary, and Jesus. They assume that because Jesus is called the
"Son of God" that this means He was God's physical son. But the Bible
does not talk at all about Jesus being the physical son of God. The idea
that God had a physical relationship with Mary that produced Jesus is
completely unfounded and exists nowhere in the Bible. In fact, the Bible
categorically rejects such thinking. The Qur'an calls this kind of belief
shirk and blasphemy (Nisaa': Surah 4 verse 48; Sincerity: Surah 112
verses 1–4).

When the Bible refers to Jesus as the Son of God, it is symbolic
language to describe the relationship of Jesus Christ to God. In Arabic,
we use similar expressions. *Ibn Sabil* means "son the road" and *'Abna'
Neel* means "sons of the Nile." Does that mean the road or the Nile have
physical children? Of course not; the language is symbolic.

The entire Bible teaches clearly the oneness of God *(tawhid)*. In
the *Tawrat* section of the Old Testament, Moses wrote: *"The LORD
our God, the LORD is one. Love the LORD your God with all your heart
and with all your soul and with all your strength"* (Deuteronomy 6:4–5,
emphasis added).

Centuries later, at the time of Christ, one of the experts on the law
(shari'a) came to Jesus and asked Him:

*"'Of all the commandments, which is the most important?' 'The most
important one,' answered Jesus, 'is this: ". . . the Lord our God, the Lord*

is one. Love the Lord your God with all your heart and with all your soul and with all your mind and with all your strength." The second is this: "Love your neighbor as yourself." There is no commandment greater than these'" (Mark 12:28–31).

The true followers of Jesus today also believe in the oneness of God *(tawhid)*. Sometimes Christians use illustrations, however inadequate, to help us grasp this complex idea. For example, H₂O is manifested as liquid (water), solid (ice), and gas (steam). Similarly, God is manifested to us in three different ways. God the creator *(Al Khalik)*, the originator of all things, has the power to create; therefore, He is called the *Father.* The very same God, not another God, has the power to speak forth His Word *(Kalimatuhu)* through *Jesus Christ.* In the Gospel of John, Jesus is called *Logos,* which is Greek for "Word" *(Kalimatuhu).* The very same God, not another, has the power to give comfort and guidance. He is the *Holy Spirit,* who is called the Comforter. God the Father is *for us,* Jesus is *with us,* and the Holy Spirit is *in us.* The Holy Spirit is not a mere force of divine power; He is the very Spirit of God. When He indwells someone, in a miraculous way God Himself actually lives in that person.

The Bible does not talk about tritheism (three gods) but about tri-unity in the oneness of His being. It is not about God, Mary, and Jesus, but about the oneness of God in the Father, His Word, and His Spirit. It is God, coming to earth in the person of His Word, Jesus, that we will look at in the rest of this chapter.

Progressive Revelation

Of all the millions of planets God created in the universe, there is one that is very special to Him. God designed earth to be the place on which He would carry out His plans with the human race. Can you imagine the Creator of the universe, the almighty God, revealing Himself to the people of this planet, beckoning them to a special relationship with Him?

When we look at the whole Bible, we see that God revealed Himself *gradually* and *progressively.* He knew the extent to which human beings could cope with His bright glory. He treated us with tenderness, revealing Himself only to the degree of our ability to cope. We do not expect someone who has been in a dark room for a long time to walk out of that room and look directly at the sun on a bright day! We expect that this person needs to adjust gradually to the light. At first he will need to wear dark sunglasses to protect himself from the bright light. This is how God exposed His bright light to mankind—very gradually.

When God appeared to Moses in the burning bush, Moses did not see Him face-to-face (Exodus 3:2). When God revealed Himself to the people of Israel in the wilderness, they saw and heard Him in lightning and thunder at the top of the mountain, but they did not see His face (Exodus 20:18). They saw His miracles repeatedly, but the Old Testament people believed that no one could see God and stay alive (Exodus 3:6, 33:20, 23).

When the Jewish temple was built in Jerusalem during the time of the Old Testament, it had three main sections. One section was for people who came to worship, another was for the priests, and the third was called the Holy of Holies. The Jews believed that the presence of God dwelt in the Holy of Holies. A big, thick curtain separated the Holy of Holies from the rest of the temple, and no one was allowed to go behind it. Only the high priest, once a year and for a very short time, went behind it to plead forgiveness for God's people. During this brief time when the high priest went behind the curtain, the people waited anxiously to see whether he would live through the experience or be struck dead.

God, in His kindness, knew our limitations as a human race and gradually gave us glimpses about Himself in creation, in the law, through the prophets, and through His intervention in people's lives. Finally, at just the right time, He visited our planet through His Word *(Kalimatuhu)*. And what a truly unique time it was. At that point in history, the Roman Empire was in control of a good part of southern Europe, the Middle East, and North Africa. They built the famous Roman roads and connected their world together. The Greek language enabled them to communicate throughout the empire. And the religion of the Jews, who lived alongside the Greeks, created an awareness of a personal God and a longing to connect with Him. At that unique time, the visit to our planet took place.

God's revelation through Christ's visit to earth was progressive and gradual as well. We see that clearly in the Gospels of Matthew, Mark, and Luke, which tell the story of Jesus' time on earth. Early on, Jesus did not want the crowds to know who He was. Over a period of three years, He gradually revealed who He was to the disciples, the men He spent the most time with. The brightness of His glory was gradually revealed according to the disciples' ability to comprehend.

This is why the visit to our planet did not occur in one week but over a period of 33 years. At the end of that period, with the events of the cross, that thick curtain in the temple that separated man from God was split in two (Matthew 27:51). That event marked a huge break-through in God's revelation of Himself to humanity. Starting on that day, mankind gained direct access to God.

THE UNIQUENESS OF JESUS

Can you imagine that God loves human beings so much that He created a special planet for us, one with air to breathe and water to drink? And He didn't make us just to be physical and social beings. He also wanted us to have spiritual capacities and inner yearnings so that we could relate to Him with intimacy. He sent prophets and gave us the law *(shari'a)* and the Scriptures, but His unique revelation came through a personal visit—He sent His Word to earth in the person of Jesus Christ. Jesus came to earth, miraculously conceived in the womb of Mary. (This is the reason why Muslims call Jesus *"Isa ibnu Mariam."*) We Arab Christians call Jesus *Yasou'*, which is closer to His Hebrew name. *Isa,* the Qur'anic name for Jesus, is closer to His Greek name. *Isa* and *Yasou'* are the same name and the same person.

Can you imagine the Word of God, Jesus, stooping down and coming to our little planet? He entered our planet not in a palace or famous city, but in an insignificant town in a country under occupation. The Word of God had to learn to read and write. He had to learn carpentry from Mary's husband, Joseph, who adopted Him. He owned everything, yet during His visit to our planet He did not own a house, a horse, or any land. He was the image of God in a human body, yet He was not recognized by the religious establishment of the time. Through Jesus *(Kalimatuhu)* all was created—the human body, plants, and animals—yet on earth He got hungry, tired, and thirsty. He was perfect and completely without sin, yet He was tempted in every way, like us, so that He could empathize with us in our weaknesses. He healed the blind and the lepers, He raised the dead, yet He chose to go in the direction of the cross.

Did anybody recognize Him for who He was? A few people did. In Matthew 16:13–20, we read that Jesus was traveling with His disciples when they reached the hills that surrounded a city called Caesarea Philippi. This was a Gentile city with many statues of gods that were worshiped by the people there. Talking with His disciples, He asked them who they thought He was:

"'Some say John the Baptist; others say Elijah; and still others, Jeremiah or one of the prophets.' 'But what about you?' he asked. 'Who do you say I am?' Simon Peter answered, 'You are the Christ, the Son of the living God.'

Jesus replied, '. . . this was not revealed to you by man, but by my Father.'"
In other words, Peter did not make this huge discovery on his own. God opened his eyes and gave him spiritual insight to know who Jesus was. Why was it so difficult for other people to recognize Jesus' true identity during His time on earth? Why is it so difficult for many people today to recognize Jesus for who He is?

Consider this illustration. Let us say that my wife and I go to the Khan El Khalili bazaar in Cairo. This bazaar is very famous, and many tourists and Egyptians visit it. Let's say it's during the time of President Reagan, a year or so after President Carter left office. As my wife and I are walking in the bazaar, I see a man wearing jeans who looks just like President Carter. I see him only for a moment before he enters one of the shops. I say to my wife, "Did you see that man? He looked very much like President Carter." My wife did not see him. Then about an hour later, we walk into a leather shop and see this man standing with a woman who looks just like Rosalyn Carter. When he sees me staring at them, he steps forward and says, "Hi, my name is Jimmy Carter." I shake his hand and say, "Man, you are good. You look just like him." Then he says to me with an emphatic voice, "I am Jimmy Carter, and this is my wife, Rosalyn." I shake her hand and say, "You look good too!"

Why is it so difficult for me to believe that this couple is the former American president and his wife? Because if this were true, the whole bazaar area would be sealed off, and nobody would be allowed inside. The place would be swarming with police and secret police. President Carter wouldn't be wearing jeans. Somehow what I saw did not match what I thought I should see. I had a "box" in my mind about how a former president would travel, and this did not fit inside my box.

Our Little Boxes

This example helps explain what happened at the time of Jesus and what still happens today. The Jews at the time of Jesus were under Roman occupation, and they were waiting for the Messiah to come rescue them. Some of the Jews were waiting for a Messiah who was a man of war who could deliver them from the Romans. Others thought he would be like a superman or a magician who could—and would—come down from the cross and prove that he was truly the Messiah. Others expected him to be recognized and endorsed by the religious establishment. Others thought that he would be rich, influential, and involved in politics. They did not expect him to be just like them, to get thirsty, hungry, or tired.

Jesus did not fit into the little boxes in their minds. He touched the lepers and was not worried about being defiled or catching their disease. Prostitutes, tax collectors, and sinners enjoyed His company. He was not aloof or distant from the common people. The religious establishment could not contain Him and claim Him as one of them. He chose the straight road that led Him to the cross, which was un-imaginable and did not make sense even to His disciples at the time. He talked about Himself and His relationship with God in a way that shocked the high priest and religious leaders. He still shocks the world today by the claims He made about Himself.

Thomas, one of His disciples, asked Him, *"'Lord, we don't know where you are going, so how can we know the way?' Jesus answered, 'I am the way and the truth and the life. No one comes to the Father except through me. If you really knew me, you would know my Father as well. From now on, you do know him and have seen him.' Philip* [another disciple] *said, 'Lord, show us the Father and that will be enough for us.' Jesus answered: 'Don't you know me, Philip, even after I have been among you such a long time? Anyone who has seen me has seen the Father'"* (John 14:5–9).

Jesus was saying to Philip: "I am God's Word and the image of the Father."

It is impossible to measure the impact Jesus' visit had on our planet. The books and songs that have been written about Him fill libraries. The people who believe in Him represent every race, language, and ethnic group. The Western calendar splits history by His birth date. He left our earth at the age of 33 and did not write one book or wage one battle, yet He left the largest impact of any human being in history. I wonder how many people in the world have seen Jesus in their dreams and visions. I wonder how many have seen the movie *The Passion of the Christ* or the movie *Jesus?* I wonder if we could count the number of people who have read the story of Jesus in the New Testament.

The more important questions for us, though, are these: Can we really believe Jesus was who He said He was? What was His purpose? What did He come to accomplish? This is what we will deal with in the next few chapters.

Earlier, when I talked about President Carter, I made the statement, "Somehow what I saw did not match what I thought I should see." How do you perceive Jesus? How would you respond to His question: "Who do you say that I am?" Ask God to deliver you from your own little boxes. Read about Him in the New Testament and ask Him to give you insight and spiritual understanding.

Reflection and Discussion Questions

1. How would you explain to another person the harmony in God being one yet having three different forms?
2. Consider the concept of God's progressive and gradual revelation of Himself to humanity. Do you see this in your life as well?
3. Is it difficult for you to believe that God was in Christ as He lived on the earth? What does it mean to you that Jesus is the image of the invisible God?
4. How do our presuppositions—our "little boxes" mentality—limit what we see? Can you think of illustrations?
5. What are your presuppositions about Christ? On what are they based?

Noteworthy:

p.30 • Progressive Revelation - revealed Himself to us to the degree we could cope

p.31 • Not a tritheism, but oneness of God the Father, His Word, and His Spirit

• Q: "Who do you say that I am?"
            -Jesus

p.31 A: "You are the Christ, the Son of the living God"
            -Peter

CHAPTER 3

THE PROOF
ABOUT JESUS

MANY PEOPLE BELIEVE THAT THERE IS NO SOLID EVIDENCE FOR THE crucifixion and the resurrection of Christ. They assume there is no proof for the authenticity of Christ as He is presented in the New Testament. At a certain time in my life, I had my doubts too. Recently, I read a book titled *The Case for Christ* by Lee Strobel, and it motivated me to write this chapter. Before writing his book, Strobel wanted to prove that any evidence for Christ could not be believed and that what the Bible said about Him was wrong. As I read this book, I kept thinking how Strobel's questions reminded me of so many of my Muslim friends' questions about Christ: Was Jesus really the person the Bible says He was? Did He really die on the cross? Can the Bible be trusted? And perhaps most important, what does Maryam: Surah 19 verse 33 mean, where Jesus talked about His own birth, death, and resurrection in the Qur'an?

BACKGROUND OF STROBEL'S BOOK

Lee Strobel, an American journalist who considered himself an atheist, wrote *The Case for Christ* in 1998. Prior to that, he worked at the well-known *Chicago Tribune* newspaper, where his specialty was covering big court cases. Before researching the book, he believed there was far more evidence that God was merely a product of wishful thinking, ancient mythology, and primitive superstition. What Jesus said about Himself, Strobel believed, was nothing more than the invention of superstitious people.

But then Strobel's wife became a follower of Christ. That stunned him, and he worried that she might become legalistic and narrow-minded. To his surprise, he noticed instead that fundamental changes took place in her character, integrity, and self-confidence. Wanting to discover what was behind these changes, he launched an all-out investigation into the facts surrounding Christ and the Bible. His search took place over a period of approximately two years. In his own words, he explains his objective this way: "Setting aside my self-interest and prejudices, as best I could, I read books, interviewed experts, asked questions, analyzed history, explored archaeology, studied ancient literature, and for the first time in my life picked apart the Bible verse by verse. I plunged into the case with more vigor than with any case I had ever pursued."[1]

With a journalist's mind, Strobel dared to ask every imaginable question as he interviewed the top experts in the world. I was amazed by the extent of his questions and by the degree to which he did not leave any stone unturned. Strobel wanted to disprove Christ, but every question he asked was fully answered. His conclusions differed radically from what he had anticipated, and he ended up writing an entire book that makes a case for Christ. My friend, if you are struggling with questions about Jesus, I encourage you to read *The Case for Christ*. Although the book is not written specifically for Muslims, I am confident that most, if not all, of your questions will be answered. Here are some of the main questions it addresses:

- Can biographies of Jesus be trusted?
- Do the biographies of Jesus stand up to scrutiny?
- Were Jesus' biographies reliably preserved for us?
- Is there credible evidence for Jesus outside His biographies?
- Does archaeology confirm or contradict Jesus' biographies?
- Is the Jesus of history the same as the Jesus of faith?
- Was Jesus really convinced that He was the Son of God?
- Was Jesus crazy when He claimed to be the Son of God?
- Did Jesus fulfill the attributes of God?
- Did Jesus—and Jesus alone—match the identity of the Messiah?
- Was Jesus' death a sham and His resurrection a hoax?
- Was Jesus' body really absent from His tomb?
- Was Jesus seen alive after His death on the cross?
- Are there any supporting facts that point to the resurrection?
- What does the evidence establish, and what does it mean today?

There is nothing wrong with honest doubt. As it did in Strobel's case, it can lead to searching and serious study, and finally it can lead to certainty. On the other hand, when people close their minds because of fear or fanaticism, they are left with only stagnation and sterile religiosity. One of

---

1 Lee Strobel, *The Case for Christ* (Grand Rapids: Zondervan, 1998), 14.

the best places to look for proof about Jesus is the Old Testament, which contains prophecies written about Christ centuries before His birth.

PROPHECIES ABOUT THE MESSIAH

The Old Testament contains nearly 50 prophecies about Jesus Christ, some of which were made centuries before His arrival on earth. The degree of exactness in these prophecies is mind-boggling. The prophet Isaiah (about 700 years before Christ) foretold that Christ would be born of a virgin. The prophet Micah (also about 700 years before Christ) prophesied that the Messiah would be born in the town of Bethlehem. The book of Genesis (about 13 centuries before Christ) and the prophet Jeremiah (about 500 years before Christ) foretold His ancestry line—that He would be a descendant of Abraham, Isaac, Jacob, from the tribe of Judah, and the house of David. The Psalms (about 800 years prior to Christ) foretold specifically His betrayal, which would take place at the hands of Judas Iscariot. The Psalms also foretold the accusations against Him, made by false witnesses.

But perhaps the most important prophecies Jesus fulfilled were those about His death and resurrection. One of the Psalms describes in detail how Christ would specifically die, yet it was written at a time when crucifixion was not even invented yet as a means of execution. The prophet Isaiah described the Messiah's suffering and death in great detail hundreds of years before they actually happened.

Some critics point out that perhaps Jesus intentionally went about fulfilling these prophecies. They claim that Jesus knew that there was a prophecy about the Messiah entering Jerusalem on a donkey, so that's what He did on that famous day, called Palm Sunday, a few days before His crucifixion. At face value, this argument looks convincing. In reality, it is weak when you take all of the prophecies into consideration. How could Jesus control the fact that Judas was paid exactly 30 pieces of silver for His betrayal, just as the prophecy says (Matthew 27:3)? How could He arrange His own ancestry to fulfill prophecy? How could He arrange to be born in the town of Bethlehem, when Mary lived in Nazareth? How could He arrange the events of His crucifixion and resurrection to match the account in the book of Isaiah?

THE REALITY OF JESUS' DEATH

What about the idea that someone else was crucified in the place of Jesus? Who could that person have been? Some believe it was Judas, who betrayed Jesus. But the Bible says that Judas was found dead after he hanged himself shortly after the crucifixion (Matthew 27:5).

If someone else was crucified in the place of Jesus, how could God punish an innocent person? If it was someone else, why didn't that person scream out that he was not the Christ? If God did not want Jesus to be crucified, couldn't He have protected Him by having Pilate declare Him innocent? If it was someone else who was crucified in Jesus' place, did this other person rise from the dead? More than 500 people saw Jesus Christ after He rose from the dead (1 Corinthians 15:6). If it was someone else who died and rose, how did that person know all those he appeared to? Why were all these people not able to differentiate between the real Jesus and that "other" person?

Some critics try to explain the resurrection by suggesting that Jesus only fainted from exhaustion on the cross or that He had been drugged, which made Him appear to have died. These critics say that after Jesus was put in a cool tomb, He was revived from the fainting spell, and thus His reappearance was not a miraculous resurrection. The tomb was empty, they say, because Jesus fled to Egypt or, as the Ahmadia sect says, He fled to India.

But what does medical science say? Is there any possibility that Jesus could have survived the torture and the crucifixion without dying?

Modern science is now able to paint a clearer picture of what happened to Jesus. For example, the Bible says that on Thursday evening, one day before the crucifixion, Jesus went with His disciples to a garden by the Mount of Olives near Jerusalem. He moved away a few feet from the disciples to pray alone. The Bible says that as He prayed, He was in a state of anguish.

"And being in anguish, he prayed more earnestly, and his sweat was like drops of blood falling to the ground" (Luke 22:44).

Is this an exaggeration, or could it be true? There is a medical condition called hematidrosis, which is associated with severe stress. The stress causes the release of chemicals that cause the breakdown of capillaries in the sweat glands. The sweat comes out tinged with blood.

As for the whipping and the torture, if you have seen the movie *The Passion of the Christ,* you will well understand what was involved. The soldiers used a leather whip with metal pieces and sharp bones woven into it. The whipping, which went all the way down from the shoulders to the back of the legs, cut the body and tore the flesh. Many who were tortured did not even live long enough to be crucified. The whipping and torture, carried out by sadistic soldiers, often resulted in death. Because of the loss of a great deal of blood, the blood pressure went down, and the kidneys stopped producing urine. The victim craved fluids because of the loss of blood. But Jesus was in excellent physical shape, and He survived the torture. The next day He had to face the cross.

The Romans used long spikes to fasten the body to the cross. The pain was excruciating, to say the least. When the cross was lifted up to a vertical position, the person's arms were stretched to the point that both shoulders were dislocated. As Jesus hung on the cross, the only way He could exhale was to push at the spike holding His feet to the cross. The agony and pain in this breathing process are unimaginable. The crucifixion was a slow, agonizing death.

For his book, Lee Strobel interviewed a medical doctor who described what Jesus must have gone through.

> As the person slows down his breathing, he goes into what is called respiratory acidosis—the carbon dioxide in the blood is dissolved as carbonic acid, causing the acidity of the blood to increase. This eventually leads to an irregular heartbeat. In fact, with his heart beating erratically, Jesus would have known that he was at the moment of death, which is when he was able to say, "Lord, into your hands I commit my spirit." And then he died of cardiac arrest.[2]

(If you want to learn more from a scientific source, see an excellent article on the death of Christ on this website: http://www.frugalsites.net/jesus/)

Because the two criminals who were crucified with Jesus had not yet died, their legs were broken so that they would suffocate. When the soldiers came to break Jesus' legs, they found that He was already dead. Just to be sure, one of them pierced His chest with a spear. The medical expert interviewed by Strobel described what happened this way:

> The spear apparently went through the right lung and into the heart, so when the spear was pulled out, some fluid—the pericardial effusion and the pleural effusion—came out. This would have the appearance of a clear fluid, like water, followed by a large volume of blood, as the eyewitness John described in his gospel.[3]

It is worth noting that Old Testament prophecies about the death of the Messiah say that none of His bones would be broken but that He

---

2 Lee Strobel, *The Case for Christ* (Grand Rapids: Zondervan, 1998), 199.
3 Ibid., 199.

would be pierced, even though the execution method of the Jews during that time was stoning.

Jesus' body was brought down from the cross, and a prominent Jewish leader asked permission to have Jesus' body so he could bury Him in his own family tomb. The burial preparations had to be done quickly because the Sabbath began that Friday night at 6 P.M. After that, no work could be done. Jesus' body was placed in the tomb, and a large boulder was placed in front of it to keep anyone from stealing the body.

Did the crucifixion, death, and burial of Christ take place, without a shadow of doubt? Yes, the evidence says it most certainly did.

AFTER THE RESURRECTION

Early on Sunday morning, some women, including Mary Magdalene, went to the tomb and discovered that Jesus' body was missing. They were told by an angel that He had been raised from the dead. For 40 days following His resurrection, Jesus appeared to various people.

He appeared to Mary Magdalene at the burial site and then to two of His followers as He walked with them on the road to Emmaus. He appeared to Peter and to the nine disciples when Thomas was not with them. When Thomas later joined them and heard the news, he did not want to believe unless he saw Jesus with his own eyes. At a later time, when the 11 disciples were together in the Upper Room and Thomas was with them, Jesus appeared to them and called Thomas to come touch His side and see His pierced hands. Thomas approached Jesus and said: *"'My Lord and my God!' Then Jesus told him, 'Because you have seen me, you have believed; blessed are those who have not seen and yet have believed'"* (John 20:28–29).

At another time, Jesus appeared to the disciples and ate with them. And still another time, He appeared to about 500 people. Finally, Jesus told His disciples to meet Him in Galilee.

"After his suffering, he showed himself to these men and gave many convincing proofs that he was alive. He appeared to them over a period of forty days and spoke about the kingdom of God. . . . He was taken up before their very eyes, and a cloud hid him from their sight" (Acts 1:3, 9).

How did the resurrection affect those closest to Jesus? After His arrest, the disciples were in disarray. Peter publicly denied Jesus three times, and the others ran away. They were afraid, intimidated, and discouraged. They thought their teacher and hero was finished, and their hopes were dashed. On Sunday morning, He rose from the dead and for 40 days appeared to them at various times, opening their eyes to understand things that He had taught them before. The resurrection of Christ transformed them from a group of cowards to a group of followers who turned the world upside down.

Peter, so cowardly during Jesus' arrest, was transformed into a courageous witness after the resurrection and after he received the Holy Spirit. He boldly proclaimed this message to a group of prominent Jews:

"'Men of Israel, listen to this: Jesus of Nazareth was a man accredited by God to you by miracles, wonders and signs, which God did among you through him, as you yourselves know. This man was handed over to you by God's set purpose and foreknowledge; and you, with the help of wicked men, put him to death by nailing him to the cross. But God raised him from the dead, freeing him from the agony of death, because it was impossible for death to keep its hold on him. . . . God has raised this Jesus to life, and we are all witnesses of the fact. . . . Therefore let all Israel be assured of this: God has made this Jesus, whom you crucified, both Lord and Christ.' When the people heard this, they were cut to the heart" (Acts 2:22–24, 32, 36–37).

Until the year A.D. 314, when Constantine made Christianity the religion of the empire, it was dangerous for people to become followers of Christ. Yet His early followers were willing to pay any cost—even torture and death—to follow Him, because their lives were so transformed by the resurrection.

What about you? Has your life been transformed by the resurrection? Are you able to believe the evidence presented here? Do you believe Jesus was who He said?

REFLECTION AND DISCUSSION QUESTIONS

1. What do you think of the idea that Jesus was not crucified and did not die? How do you reconcile that idea with what Jesus said about His birth, death, and resurrection in Maryam: Surah 19 verse 33 and Al Umran: Surah 3 verse 55?
2. What do you think of the prophecies about the Savior and their fulfillment in Jesus?
3. Have you seen the movies *Jesus* and *The Passion of the Christ*? Do you think they accurately portray what happened to Jesus on Thursday night and on the following day when He was crucified?
4. Are you able to buy the argument that someone else died in Jesus' place and was raised from the dead? Is there anything about this theory that you find hard to believe?
5. What does the resurrection of Christ mean to you? Does it have a practical impact on your life? NoteWoRthy:

(p37-39) • Lee Strobel - Atheist journalist → Case for Christ ("Nothing wrong with honest doubt")
(p.39) • Prophecies
(p.40-49) • Post-Resurrection transformation of followers.

CHAPTER 4

THE LADDER

MENTALITY

AN EGYPTIAN FRIEND OF MINE ONCE TOLD ME ABOUT A DEPRESSING painting he had seen. It was a religious painting of a long ladder extending from earth to the gates of heaven. On this long ladder, a few people were climbing steadily upward. The higher they were on the ladder, the more devout and religious they looked. What was discouraging about this painting, though, were the many people falling off the ladder. The most discouraging part to my friend was the fact that the "saint" who almost reached the top of the ladder had fallen and was diving down. That painting did not give my friend hope that people can make it into heaven. People who perceive the law as a long ladder they must climb to please God and earn His acceptance do not offer much hope to our world.

When my family lived in Egypt, I had a Muslim friend who lived in our neighborhood. In fact, he was one of the most devout Muslims I have ever known. We used to get together once a week to talk and read about God. Every day for many years, he prayed the five prayers. For the dawn prayer or prayer at sunrise, he used to go to the nearby mosque, even in the cold winter months.

During that time, I visited New Zealand and met some Middle Eastern Muslim immigrants who were very legalistic in how they practiced Islam. They felt they were following God's commands to the letter and that they were pleasing Him. So I shared with them about my humble and devout friend in Cairo who prayed the five prayers every day for years. I also told them that ever since he was a child, he fasted every day of every Ramadan month; not only that, he fasted every Friday for years. To my surprise, they responded, "Unless he fasted on Thursdays as well, fasting on Friday does not count." Their legalistic calculations made me wonder. What is their view of God? What is their view of the law and its purpose? These people seemed to have a very long ladder to climb.

In the Arabic Bible, the word for law is *shari'a* or *namous*. This word is not restricted to Muslim use only. The law, or *shari'a*, is a major element in most world religions. In all of these religions, there is a big temptation to focus on the letter of the law, which can lead to a burdensome life of legalism. Legalists end up in shackles, missing out on intimacy with God. For them, worship is conducted out of duty *(fard)* rather than love.

Rabi'a Al Adawiya, a Muslim mystic, is one of my heroes. She was a slave who was set free because of her walk with God. She became such a famous Muslim woman of God that many women asked her to mentor them. In time, she started something similar to a convent for Muslim women. In one of her famous prayers, she said something like this to God: *Lord, why do I love you? Do I love you out of a desire to go to paradise? If this is my motive, then deprive me of paradise. Or do I love you out of fear of going to hell? If this is my motive, then send me to hell. O Lord, please purify my motives. Help me to love you for your own sake because you are worthy of all my love and all my worship.*[1]

This fantastic Muslim woman was motivated by love rather than duty *(fard)*.

THE LAW BEFORE THE TIME OF CHRIST

There were legalistic Jews, before the coming of Christ, who missed out on the real meaning and intention of the law. Today, members of all religions still miss out on the purpose of the law. I can relate to this. As a Christian, I once struggled with my own legalism, holding a checklist mentality of trying to please God. It was a burden. But over the years, I have learned more and more to enjoy living in an atmosphere of grace rather than being shackled by a misunderstanding of the purpose of the law.

In one of his New Testament letters, the apostle Paul described his Jewish background before his encounter with Christ and how he struggled with the law. Through an encounter with Christ, he became unshackled.

"I tried keeping rules and working my head off to please God, and it didn't work. So I quit being a 'law man' [legalist] so that I could be God's man. Christ's life showed me how, and enabled me to do it. I identified myself completely with him. Indeed, I have been crucified with Christ. My

---

1 Paraphrased from *Waging Peace on Islam* by Christine Mallouhi (London: Monarch Books, 2000), 292.

ego is no longer central. It is no longer important that I appear righteous before you or have your good opinion, and I am no longer driven to impress God. Christ lives in me. The life you see me living is not 'mine,' but it is lived by faith in the Son of God, who loved me and gave himself for me. . . . If a living relationship with God could come by rule keeping, then Christ died unnecessarily" (Galatians 2:19–21, *The Message*).

If we look at the whole Old Testament, we find a total of 613 laws. They are an expansion of what is known as the Ten Commandments, found in Exodus 20:1–17. These laws are basic moral teachings that find parallels in most world religions. Here they are by their numbers:

1. You shall have no other gods before me.
2. You shall not make for yourself an idol. You shall not bow down to them or worship them.
3. You shall not misuse the name of the Lord your God.
4. Remember the Sabbath day by keeping it holy.
5. Honor your father and your mother.
6. You shall not murder.
7. You shall not commit adultery.
8. You shall not steal.
9. You shall not give false testimony.
10. You shall not covet.

Before the time of Christ, some of the Jews were zealous to obey the law to the letter, even though they misunderstood its purpose and intent. These zealous Jews were so worried about breaking any of the specific Ten Commandments—or any of the 613 laws in general—that they started adding additional laws as lines of defense. How could the additional laws, which numbered more than 1,500, protect the original 613 laws from being broken? Think about this illustration.

Suppose I were a person who spent several hours every day watching TV. Then let's say I come to my senses one day and repent about my lifestyle and determine that for a whole month I will not watch TV. I even disconnect the TV and put it in its box. During this month, for sure, I would find myself with extra hours every day to do things I never had time for in the past. So I visit friends. I read books, read my Bible more frequently, and work on my hobbies. A few weeks into this, I begin wondering if I should keep the TV disconnected forever so that I can live my life in a richer, fuller way.

What do you think would be my favorite topic when I talked with friends and coworkers? Of course, it would be the TV and how my whole life turned around when I got unshackled from it. By saying this, I am consciously or unconsciously telling people, *"Thou shall not watch TV."* This "commandment" is not in my book, but I add it as a line of defense. Over time, those who follow my preaching would come to the petrified conclusion that watching TV is sin. They would end up being shackled by a law God never intended.

Look around you, my friend. Among your religious friends and relatives, do you see free people, or do you see shackled people who are trying to climb a very long ladder with no assurance they can make it to the top? Without understanding the real purposes of the law, this is where we can easily end up.

The Pharisees of Jesus' Day

At the time of Christ, the Pharisees had an elaborate system of scrupulous observances and ordinances to help them climb their daily ladder. To practice and obey the law, which had more than 1,500 extra laws that are not in the Bible, a person had to be a full-time ladder-climber. He also had to be rich; anyone with a regular job could not practice the time-consuming observance of the law. Even going out shopping would cause the Pharisee to become defiled. If a woman who was having her period sat on a chair, that chair and everything else the woman touched became defiled. Can you imagine those frustrated Pharisees, trying to stay ceremonially clean when everything around them was full of defilement *(najasa)*? With this mind-set, the Pharisees found it convenient to compare themselves with less "pure" people. They looked down at those below them on the ladder and at those who were not able to even start climbing. As they made this comparison, they became conceited and self-righteous.

How does the Bible describe the Pharisees?

"The Pharisees and all the Jews do not eat unless they give their hands a ceremonial washing, holding to the tradition of the elders. When they come from the marketplace they do not eat unless they wash [ceremonial washing]. *And they observe many other traditions, such as the* [ceremonial] *washing of cups, pitchers and kettles"* (Mark 7:3–4).

This is what Jesus said about the Pharisees: *"'You have let go of the commands of God* [the Ten Commandments and the way they are expanded in the 613 laws] *and are holding on to the traditions of men* [the 1,500 additional laws]'"* (Mark 7:8).

Jesus saw through the hypocrisy of these people and challenged them at every turn. To those who tried to impress others by the way they prayed or by their devout appearance, He said: *"And when you pray, do not be like the hypocrites, for they love to pray standing . . . on the street corners to be seen by men'"* (Matthew 6:5).

And to those who tried to show off when they were fasting by having long faces, He said: *"'When you fast, do not look somber as the hypocrites do, for they disfigure their faces to show men they are fasting'"* (Matthew 6:16). Jesus challenged these hypocrites.

"'Everything they do is done for men to see. . . . Woe to you, teachers of the law and Pharisees, you hypocrites! You shut the kingdom of heaven in men's faces. You yourselves do not enter, nor will you let those enter who are trying to. Woe to you, teachers of the law and Pharisees, you hypocrites! You travel over land and sea to win a single convert, and when he becomes one, you make him twice as much a son of hell as you are. . . . Woe to you, teachers of the law and Pharisees, you hypocrites! You clean the outside of the cup and dish, but inside they are full of greed and self-indulgence. Blind Pharisee! First clean the inside of the cup and dish, and then the outside also will be clean. Woe to you, teachers of the law and Pharisees, you hypocrites! You are like whitewashed tombs, which look beautiful on the outside but on the inside are full of dead men's bones and everything unclean. In the same way, on the outside you appear to people as righteous but on the inside you are full of hypocrisy and wickedness'" (Matthew 23:5, 13–15, 25–28).

God evaluates people not based on their *outward appearances* and rigorous religiosity but on their *inner purity*. God looks at our hearts rather than at how well we are climbing the ladder.

Two Ways of Living

One of my favorite Surahs in the Qur'an is Al Fatiha: Surah 1. To Muslims, *Al Fatiha* is as important as the "Lord's Prayer" is to Christians. In this Surah, which is recited in ceremonial prayers and on many other occasions, there is a prayer, *"Ihdina Al-Sirat Al Mustaqim"* ("Guide us on the straight road."). *"Al-Sirat"* is an ancient Arabic word that is translated in the Qur'an as "road," "path," or "way." The prayer, "Lead us, or guide us, on the straight road," should not be the prayer of Muslims only but of every person who desires to have a deep intimacy with God.

How can we move on that right path, road, or way? I believe there are two options. One way is to follow the ladder mentality, worshiping God out of duty *(fard)* and assuming that we are satisfying Him through our good works and our righteousness *(al bir wal ihsan)*. Some Muslims imagine this "straight road" as a bridge over a river of fire, which is as narrow as a hair and as sharp as a sword's edge.

The other way is to worship God out of love instead of duty.

To understand the difference between these options, consider these illustrations. Some years ago, a family went to the airport in a small American city to meet their friends who were arriving at 9:30 P.M. When they reached the airport, they found that the plane would be 90 minutes late. So this family of four—a father, a mother, and two children—decided to wait at the airport. The daughter was about 5 years old, and the boy was a toddler who was just learning how to walk. The little girl wanted to play on the descending escalator as they waited. Because there was hardly anybody at the airport at that time, her parents allowed her to play. For about 15 minutes, she tried unsuccessfully to climb the descending escalator, until she got bored and stopped playing.

This illustration describes people from all religions who have a ladder mentality, who are motivated by duty *(fard)* and by a desire to practice righteousness *(al bir wal ihsan)* to earn God's acceptance. They are, metaphorically speaking, climbing a descending escalator. But they are not like that little girl who played for only 15 minutes before tiring of this activity. They are stuck climbing day in and day out, every day of their lives. Secular people tend to go up slowly on the descending escalator because they believe that the escalator is going down slowly. Secular Muslims tend to be lax in their practice of religion because they think that God does not demand a great deal. Committed fundamentalists, on the other hand, tend to run up the descending escalator because they believe that it is going down fast. The sad thing, though, is that both groups, secular and fundamentalist, are not sure whether they can make it to the top or not. Only if God bestows His mercy on them and plucks them off the escalator as they go through the process of death can they make it into paradise.

Let us return to that family at the airport. They went up to the second floor, the departure level. In those days, before 9/11, people could walk all the way to the gates to meet their friends. On the way to the gate was a moving walkway about 50 meters long. The father wanted to play with his little boy who was learning to walk. He asked his wife to place their son at the start of the moving walkway, and then he went to the end of the walkway. The father looked at his little boy, and with a big smile and wide-open arms, he called his son by name and told him, "Come." The little boy looked at his dad, smiled, and started walking toward him on the moving walkway. He was wobbly and fell down. So the father called out to him and with a big smile said, "It is OK. Get up.

Come." When the boy heard the voice of his dad and saw his smile and wide-open arms, he got up, stopped crying, and started walking toward his dad again. After a short time, the boy stopped walking and stood staring at a bright yellow sign. He forgot that his dad existed, yet he was still carried toward him by the moving walkway. Then he heard his dad calling him, remembered that his dad was there, and started to walk toward him once again.

The first scenario, *the descending escalator,* is a ladder mentality. A person is motivated by duty and ends up in shackles. The second scenario, *the moving walkway,* illustrates life with Jesus as He moves us along the "straight road." Notice that being on the moving walkway requires both discipline and grace. Discipline is necessary—the little boy must practice walking and using his muscles. Life on this moving walkway is not lazy. But there is also grace on the moving walkway. Even when the little boy fell down—even when he forgot the purpose of being on the moving walkway—he was still being carried by grace.

My friend, where are you? Are you tired of climbing a descending escalator? Are you attracted to the moving walkway? In the next chapters, we will look at how to get on the moving walkway and how to continue moving forward on it.

Reflection and Discussion Questions

1. Do you think the Ten Commandments can be fully followed and obeyed on a daily basis? Why did God give the Ten Commandments? What do you think is the purpose of the law?
2. Why do people tend to accumulate more and more laws and get shackled with them? Does this happen today?
3. Can you think of people, Muslims or Christians, who are climbing a descending escalator?
4. Have you noticed anyone whose lifestyle indicates they are living on the moving walkway? What is it about them that makes you think they are on the moving walkway?

CHAPTER 5

THE PASSING GRADE

WHEN I WAS IN COLLEGE, THE PASSING GRADE AT MY UNIVERSITY
was 60 percent. Placing the grades on a curve was an innovation that
we loved. The best grade in the class, whether 50 percent or 95 percent,
became 100 percent, and all the other scores fell in line accordingly.
This meant that as long as I was doing better than most everyone else in
the class, my grade would be good.

What do you think is the passing grade with God? On what basis
will He accept us? How can we know whether our efforts are good
enough? Does God grade on a curve, in which case I don't need to be
perfect, just a little better than everyone else? Am I safe because my
sins are less evil than the sins of those who are in high-security prisons?
How does God evaluate me? What satisfies Him?

GOD'S STANDARDS

If we look at the five books of the Bible written by Moses *(Tawarat)*, we
find extensive teaching on the law *(shari'a)*. After the people of Israel
left Egypt under the leadership of Moses, they wandered for about 40
years in the wilderness because of their stubbornness and disobedience.
The older generation died, except for a handful of individuals, and Moses knew that his time of death was coming soon. The people of Israel
were at the east side of the Jordan River, ready to cross over and enter
the land of Canaan, their new home. Moses wanted to teach this new
generation the law and give them, as it were, his last will and testament.
It was his final opportunity to help his people get on the straight road.
He taught them the law so they would know how to live in a way that
was acceptable to God.

To me, the shocking part of his teaching comes in Deuteronomy 28.
In the first two verses, Moses says this: *"If you fully obey the LORD your
God and carefully follow all his commands I give you today, the LORD your
God will set you high above all the nations on earth. All these blessings*

will come upon you and accompany you if you obey the LORD *your God'"* (Deuteronomy 28:1–2).

The verses that follow, verses 3–14, enumerate the various blessings that the people of God would experience if they fulfilled the condition. What was the condition? *"If you* fully obey . . . *and carefully follow* all *his commands"* (emphasis added). Then comes verse 15: *"However, if you do not obey the* LORD *your God and do not carefully follow all his commands and decrees I am giving you today, all these curses will come upon you and overtake you.'"*

Starting with verse 16 and continuing until the end of the chapter— and it is a very long chapter, ending in verse 68—we see the enumeration of curses on those who fail to fulfill the conditions. What are the conditions? *"If you* do not obey *the* LORD *your God and do not carefully follow* all *his commands"* (emphasis added). I don't know how many of the 613 Old Testament laws were revealed by that time, but what God required was *full and total* obedience to *all* the commandments.

God placed Adam in the Garden of Eden and gave him the freedom to eat all the fruit in the Garden except the fruit from one tree. Adam had a hard time obeying just that one commandment. Imagine trying to obey all 613. Furthermore, God's passing grade is not 60 or 80 percent, or even 99 percent. Nothing satisfies God's absolute standards except full and total obedience—a 100 percent grade. This looks very dim and discouraging. Can anyone fulfill these difficult, even impossible, conditions? And what are the consequences if we can't?

THE CONSEQUENCES

At the end of the Bible, in Revelation 20:11–15, we get a vivid description of what will happen on the Day of Judgment. Here is the text from the Bible with my comments in brackets:

"Then I saw a great white throne and him who was seated on it. [This is a description of God sitting on His throne on the Day of Judgment.] . . . *And I saw the dead, great and small, standing before the throne, and books were opened.* [Note that the word "books" is plural rather than singular.] *Another book was opened* [This time it is a singular book.]*, which is the book of life. The dead were judged according to what they had done as recorded in the books.* [It appears that there is an accurate record kept of every sin committed by every human that is revealed on the Day of Judgment. This record is in the form of a book for each person.] . . . *And each person was judged according to what he had done.* [No one will escape judgment, and it will be fair, as each person will

be judged according to what he/she has done, what has been written in that person's book.] . . . *If anyone's name was not found written in the book of life, he was thrown into the lake of fire.* [These are the consequences of not getting a 100 percent grade.]"

This is the fate of all who have been trying to climb the *descending escalator*, whether they are Jew, Christian, Muslim, Hindu, or secular. No matter how good they have been, no matter how hard they tried to climb that ladder by decreasing their sins and increasing their good works, they still sin, and an account is kept of every sin they committed.

I thought of this as I was visiting a U.S. university a few years ago. I met an Egyptian Ph.D. student there who was happy and satisfied with his religiosity while living in America. Because it was right after Ramadan, I asked him about his fasting and his five daily prayers. He proudly reported that he fasted 27 days of the month. As for his five daily prayers, he rationalized and made excuses, telling me that living in America is not like living in Egypt, where most people fast and pray. He told me how hard it is to be religious and do all that is required by God because it takes so much time.

I said to him, "Suppose you were a very good man, doing your duties to the maximum, fasting and praying. And because you are a very good man, God only counts against you 10 sins a day. But because God is so merciful and compassionate, He reduces the number of sins against you to only 3 sins a day. How big will your book be on the Day of Judgment? If only 3 sins are counted against you each day, then you will have 21 sins counted against you per week, which is more than 1,000 sins counted against you each year. If you live to the age of 70, your book will be very thick, recording at least 70,000 sins. How can you stand before the almighty God, the Judge, on that day?"

As this Egyptian student faced the ugly reality, he responded in panic by saying: "God does not count the sins of children. He looks at their lies as white lies." So I asked him, "Until what age?" He answered, "Until the age of 10 or 12." "OK," I told him, "Your book will have 58,000 sins."

For people who live their lives trying to increase their good deeds on one side of the scale and to reduce their sins on the other side, it does not look hopeful. The question is not how much do we sin, but *do we sin at all?* Climbing a descending escalator, day in and day out, year after year, is a heavy and fruitless burden. Relating with God out of duty *(fard)* is a hard, monotonous way of life. Furthermore, the consequences on the Day of Judgment are terrifying. Is there a better option? Yes! And we see it in the second part of the text we read from Revelation.

The second option offered is this: *"If anyone's name was not found written in the book of life, he was thrown into the lake of fire."* Reversing this phrase tells us that all those whose names were written in the Book of Life had their own book destroyed. They were no longer under condemnation. Because their names were written in the Book of Life, these people were on the straight road, the moving walkway. How can you get your name in the Book of Life? We will find out in the coming chapters. But first we need to address how Jesus related to the law.

Jesus and the Law

The law (*shari'a*) in the Old Testament covered many categories, including:

- Civil laws regarding government and leadership. In Islam, one of these types of laws is called *Khilafa* (successors of the Prophet).
- Dietary laws, such as what is kosher for the Jews (called *haram* and *halal* by Muslims).
- The Sabbath (unique to Judaism).
- Diseases and how to deal with sicknesses, including leprosy.
- Clean and unclean. This area of the law shares great similarities with the *shari'a* in Islam, as it addresses how to get clean and stay clean (*tahara* and *najasa*).
- Social relationships such as marriage and divorce.
- The house of faith, or insiders versus outsiders. Jews referred to outsiders as "Gentiles."
- One final category is very important in the Old Testament and has no parallels in any other religion except for Christianity. It has to do with the laws regarding sacrifices and the sacrificial system. In Islam there is a record of Abraham, in obedience to God, being willing to offer his son as a sacrifice. It is called the Great Sacrifice (*Al thabh al 'azeem* in Al-Saffat: Surah 37 verse 107). But the whole sacrificial system *(Kaffara)* is not as central in Islam as it is in Judaism and Christianity.

Jesus grew up under the law just as all the Jews of that time did. But when Jesus began His public ministry, He said this about the law: *"Do not think that I have come to abolish the Law or the Prophets; I have not come to abolish them but to fulfill them"* (Matthew 5:17).

Jesus related to the law in a number of ways:

- When it came to rigid external commands, Jesus said: *"'You have let go of the commands of God* [the Ten Commandments as they are expounded in the 613 laws] *and are holding on to the traditions of men* [the 1,500 additional laws]'" (Mark 7:8). Another way of saying this is, "You have held fast and rigidly to the letter of the law and let go of the heart and intent of the law."

- Jesus pointed out the deeper issues rather than the externals. For example, the Pharisees were very concerned about the ceremonial washings and eating only what was clean *(halal)*. Jesus said to them: *"'Listen to me, everyone, and understand this. Nothing outside a man can make him "unclean" by going into him. Rather, it is what comes out of a man that makes him "unclean." For from within, out of men's hearts, come evil thoughts, sexual immorality, theft, murder, adultery, greed, malice, deceit, lewdness, envy, slander, arrogance and folly. All these evils come from inside and make a man "unclean"'"* (Mark 7:14–15, 21–23). Jesus focused on inner cleanliness, cleanliness of the heart.

- When it came to the moral law, Jesus helped His followers understand the intent of the law rather than just obeying it out of duty *(fard)*. He spoke with authority—not as a prophet, but as a person who is greater than a prophet. He said: *"'You have heard that it was said, "Eye for eye, and tooth for tooth." But I tell you, Do not resist an evil person. If someone forces you to go one mile, go with him two miles. Give to the one who asks you, and do not turn away from the one who wants to borrow from you'"* (Matthew 5:38–39, 41–42).

- When it came to disciplines of obedience, Jesus focused on the love relationship with God rather than on the duties we must perform to please God. A Jewish teacher of the law asked Jesus which of God's commandments was the most important. Jesus answered: *"'The Lord is one. Love the Lord your God with all your heart and with all your soul and with all your mind and with all your strength'"* (Mark 12:29–30).

- When it came to the sacrificial system, Jesus brought completely new meaning. The Old Testament sacrificial system was detailed and elaborate. The books of the law of Moses, including Exodus, Leviticus, and Numbers, teach extensively on the types of offerings and sacrifices the Jews were to make. There were priests dedicated to serving God by following the exact demands of the law regarding sacrifices. The temple must have looked and smelled like a slaughterhouse as bulls, sheep, and other animals were sacrificed precisely and continually. These Old Testament sacrifices serve to *foreshadow Christ's crucifixion.* Jesus, once and for all, became "The Sacrifice." He fulfilled the law by being the perfect sacrifice.

PURPOSES OF THE LAW

If the law is impossible to fulfill—if it could only be fulfilled through the person of Jesus Christ—why did God give it to His people? Why does the law exist in all religions? The following few verses in the New Testament give a good summary of the purposes of the law.

- It served as a babysitter or guardian until we reach the age of maturity. *"Before this faith came, we were held prisoners by the law, locked up until faith should be revealed. So the law was put in charge to lead us to Christ that we might be justified by faith. Now that faith has come, we are no longer under the supervision of the law"* (Galatians 3:23–25). The law was an important guardian, preparing us for Christ's visit to our planet. Once Christ came, that purpose of the law was fulfilled and finished.

- It was a reminder. *"But those sacrifices are an annual reminder of sins, because it is impossible for the blood of bulls and goats to take away sins"* (Hebrews 10:3–4). As the Jews followed closely the ceremonial law and regularly offered their sacrifices, they were constantly reminded of their sin and their need for God's forgiveness. The sacrifices reminded them that they could not earn the 100 percent passing grade and that they constantly needed God's forgiveness through the sacrificial system.

- It acted as a mirror or a measuring tape. *"Therefore no one will be declared righteous in his sight by observing the law; rather, through the law we become conscious of sin"* (Romans 3:20). Suppose that I was working on my car and my hands got dirty and greasy; then, without knowing it, I touched my face. If I did not look at the mirror, I might never guess that my face was dirty. When we frequently look at the Ten Commandments, we become sensitive to seeing sin in our lives. If there is no "mirror" to see what is right and what is wrong, people become callous and socially deviant.

- The law leads people to despair about their own efforts and to develop a sense of being unworthy of God's mercy and grace. *"The law was added so that the trespass* [awareness of sin] *might increase"* (Romans 5:20). Jesus put this principle into a parable. He said, *"To some who were confident of their own righteousness and looked down on everybody else, Jesus told this parable: 'Two men went up to the temple to pray, one a Pharisee and the other a tax collector. The Pharisee stood up and prayed about himself: "God, I thank you that I am not like other men—robbers, evildoers, adulterers—or even like this tax collector. I fast twice a week and give a tenth of all I get." But the tax collector stood at a distance. He would not even look up to heaven, but beat his breast and said, "God, have mercy on me, a sinner." I tell you that this man, rather than the other, went home justified before God"* (Luke 18:9–14).

The Pharisee saw himself "at the top of the ladder." He looked down at others with an attitude of self-righteousness and pride. He thought that he was earning God's acceptance through his religiosity. In contrast, the tax collector felt unworthy of stepping into the temple because he was very much aware of his sinfulness and unworthiness. In this story, the law accomplished its purpose with the tax collector but not with the Pharisee.

Do you find yourself climbing a ladder, my friend, trying to earn the acceptance of God? Have you convinced yourself consciously or unconsciously that God will grade you on a curve—that as long as you are not as bad as some people are, you are "safe"? I hope that what you have read in this chapter has opened your eyes to that faulty way of thinking. Remember that being honest with yourself is the key to having an encounter with God.

REFLECTION AND DISCUSSION QUESTIONS

1. If the passing grade to satisfy God's absolute standards is nothing less than 100 percent, what is the solution?
2. What are the various purposes of the law? How have you experienced some of these purposes of the law in your life?
3. Is it possible to have an attitude similar to that of the tax collector (Luke 18:9–14) without having to commit many sins? What does it take to develop an attitude of being unworthy?
4. How do you see the law as a stage in God's progressive revelation of Himself to humanity?

CHAPTER 6

GOING BEHIND

THE LAW

A FEW YEARS AGO, I WAS VISITING A MUSLIM COUNTRY AND MET A professor from the main university in the capital city. I was surprised to learn that he was a professor and that he was married with children because he looked very young. Actually, he looked more like a student. This professor told me about an experience he had a few years earlier when Mr. Ahmad Didaat visited their university.

Mr. Didaat, who died in 2005, was a South African of Indian descent and had written many books attacking Christianity and the Bible. Mr. Didaat was invited by the Muslim association at that university to come give a lecture to the student body on Islam and Christianity. The young professor that I met, who was a committed follower of Christ, attended the lecture along with a few Christian students. Among Mr. Didaat's many harsh attacks on Christianity was one aimed at what is called the Sermon on the Mount, which is recorded in Matthew chapters 5, 6, and 7. Mr. Didaat claimed that Christ's teachings were unrealistic and that they were an impossible ladder to climb; therefore, they were useless. Finally, he challenged any Christians in the audience to prove that Christ's teachings are worth following. The Christian professor accepted the challenge, and he joined Mr. Didaat on the stage. Everyone in the lecture hall knew who the professor was except Mr. Didaat, who assumed that he was a student. Because he thought the professor was a student, he made no attempt to be polite and respectful.

Mr. Didaat read to him Jesus' words from Matthew 5:38–48.

"'You have heard that it was said, "Eye for eye, and tooth for tooth."
But I tell you, Do not resist an evil person. If someone strikes you on the
right cheek, turn to him the other also. And if someone wants to sue you
and take your tunic, let him have your cloak as well. If someone forces you
to go one mile, go with him two miles. Give to the one who asks you, and

do not turn away from the one who wants to borrow from you. You have heard that it was said, "Love your neighbor and hate your enemy." But I tell you: Love your enemies and pray for those who persecute you, that you may be sons of your Father in heaven. He causes his sun to rise on the evil and the good, and sends rain on the righteous and the unrighteous. If you love those who love you, what reward will you get? Are not even the tax collectors doing that? And if you greet only your brothers, what are you doing more than others? Do not even pagans do that? Be perfect, therefore, as your heavenly Father is perfect."

Mr. Didaat focused on verse 40: "*If someone wants to sue you and take your tunic, let him have your cloak as well.*" He asked the professor to give him his shirt. The students were shocked by the rudeness with which their professor was being treated. But the professor took off his shirt and gave it to him. Then Mr. Didaat asked the professor to give him his trousers as well—you know this is difficult in Muslim societies. But after asking the female students to close their eyes, he took off his trousers and gave them to Mr. Didaat. One of the male students was so embarrassed that he ran to the stage and gave his jacket to the professor. The professor wrapped the jacket around his waist and then reached for the microphone. He told Mr. Didaat that he was a professor at this university and that he was being treated very rudely by him. If my memory serves me right, Mr. Didaat was blacklisted and never allowed to visit that country again.

Was the professor living out the Sermon on the Mount by giving his shirt and trousers to Mr. Didaat? Is that the intent of what Jesus was saying? No. By doing these things, the professor earned the right to be heard as he shared about the intent of the law, which is really the important part of Jesus' sermon. We should focus on the attitudes and the motivations behind the law when we study the Sermon on the Mount. We'll understand this more as we take a closer look at the purposes of the law.

PURPOSES OF THE LAW

In the previous chapter, I talked about the purposes of the law. Here is a short summary:

- The law was a *babysitter* or a *guardian* until we reach the age of maturity (Galatians 3:23–25). The law guarded us and prepared us for Christ's arrival on earth. Once Christ came, that purpose of the law was fulfilled and finished.
- The law was a *reminder* (Hebrews 10:3–4). As the Jews closely followed the ceremonial law and offered their sacrifices regularly, they were constantly reminded of their sin and their need for

God's forgiveness. The sacrifices reminded them that they could not earn the 100 percent passing grade.

- The law was a *mirror* or a *measuring tape* (Romans 3:20). When we look at the Ten Commandments, we become sensitive to seeing sin in our lives. If there is no "mirror" or "measuring tape" telling us what is right and what is wrong, people become calloused and socially deviant.
- The law leads people to *despair about their own efforts* and to develop a sense of unworthiness of God's mercy and grace (Romans 5:20).

The entire text of the Sermon on the Mount (Matthew 5, 6, and 7) is included in Appendix A of this book. Before you move to the next chapter, please go to the end of the book and do the Bible study there. Try to look for the purposes of the law revealed in this "sermon." Meditate on it and try to respond either individually or in a small group to the questions presented at the end of the study.

SURPASSING THE LAW

Much like the traffic laws of today, many of the Old Testament religious civil laws dealt with conduct and behavior rather than with attitudes and motives. Traffic violations are not measured by the intention of the person but by how fast he was driving and what laws he has broken. These laws are minimal and serve as a *babysitter* or a *guardian,* preparing us for the heart and intent of the law.

In the Sermon on the Mount, we see not the minimum law but a *surpassing* of the law. Jesus did not abolish the Old Testament law; rather, He showed us what is behind it and invited us to aim higher. Jesus said in Matthew 5:17, *"Do not think that I have come to abolish the Law or the Prophets; I have not come to abolish them but to fulfill them,"* and He did. He revealed to us the intent of the law and focused on motives and attitudes rather than on conduct and behavior.

For example, rather than addressing adultery, a behavior, He addressed the source of adultery. He said in Matthew 5:27–28, *"You have heard that it was said, 'Do not commit adultery.' But I tell you that anyone who looks at a woman lustfully has already committed adultery with her in his heart."*

If the focus is on the behavior only and not on the source of the behavior, which has to do with motives, then a person could easily become like the Pharisees, whom Jesus described this way: *"Hypocrites! You are like whitewashed tombs, which look beautiful on the outside but on the inside are full of dead men's bones and everything unclean"* (Matthew 23:27).

Jesus invited us to the heart of the law and to a focus on the inner being and character rather than the externals.

Another purpose of the law was to remind us of our sins and our need for forgiveness. When we look at the Sermon on the Mount, we do not see a God who is a harsh judge, making us jump through hoops to please Him. The Sermon on the Mount shows us what God is really like. He is righteous and compassionate. The sermon draws us to God and to His absolute standards and gives us a realistic estimate of who He is and who we are.

Still another purpose of the law was to be a mirror or a measuring stick that shows us what we are really like. If the mirror is cracked, it will fail to show us the details of what we are really like. If the measuring stick is made of rubber and can be stretched, it will fail to accurately measure. If the spiritual laws are diluted to match our ability to live up to them, like Mr. Didaat thought, then these laws have lost their ability to awaken our consciences.

Civil laws should deal with the minimum requirements that allow people to live with mutual respect and consideration for one another. These laws should protect us from things like traffic accidents and stealing from one another. Spiritual laws, on the other hand, draw us to what God is like and far surpass the civil laws. In the Sermon on the Mount, God's absolute standards are revealed, and we see who we really are and what we are like. As we look at the perfect mirror, we see our true selves without deception or compromise. In aiming at His perfect and absolute standards, we move in our pursuit of holiness.

When working on their shooting skills, beginners as well as professional shooters aim at the bull's-eye. The beginners are not encouraged to shoot at the outer rims just because they are beginners. Like the pros, the beginners are trained to aim for the bull's-eye, the center of the target. Without absolute standards, everything becomes relative, and people do what looks good in their own eyes.

Another major purpose of the law is to help us realistically see our depravity, shame, and defilement *(najasa)* and give up on the false notion that we can satisfy the absolute demands of God. Unless we *despair of our efforts* to climb the descending escalator, we will never be ready to accept God's gracious offer of forgiveness and full acceptance.

When we focus on the law as a ladder that we can climb, we become self-centered in our rigorous religiosity, and our perception of God is marred. If, on the other hand, we see what God is really like—His righteousness and compassion—then we are humbled before Him. We despair of our attempts to earn His acceptance and fall on our knees before Him in true submission. This is the meaning of the word "Islam."

THE BEATITUDES

The Sermon on the Mount has always held the first place of attention and esteem among the sayings of Jesus. The most difficult part of the sermon is a section called the Beatitudes, which are the first few verses of the sermon. The *International Standard Bible Encyclopedia* says this about the Sermon on the Mount:

> Unlike many reformers, Jesus begins the exposition of His program with a promise of happiness, with a blessing rather than a curse. He thus connects His program directly with the hopes of His hearers, for the central features in the current Messianic conception were deliverance and happiness. But the conditions of happiness proposed were in strong contrast with those in the popular thought. Happiness does not consist, says Jesus, in what one possesses, in lands and houses, in social position, in intellectual attainments, but in the wealth of the inner life, in moral strength, in self-control, in spiritual insight, in the character one is able to form within himself and in the service he is able to render to his fellowmen. Happiness, then, like character, is a by-product of right living. It is presented as the fruit, not as the object of endeavor.
>
> It is interesting to note that character is the secret of happiness both for the individual and for society. There are two groups of Beatitudes. The first four deal with personal qualities: humility, penitence, self-control, desire for righteousness. These are the sources of inner peace. The second group deals with social qualities; mercifulness toward others, purity of heart or reverence for personality, peacemaking or solicitude for others, self-sacrificing loyalty to righteousness. These are the sources of social rest. The blessings of the kingdom are social as well as individual.[1]

The following, *in italics,* are the actual words of Jesus as they appear in Matthew 5:3–12. I have paraphrased each one (with the help of Arabic commentaries) to help you understand what Jesus said.

1 *International Standard Bible Encyclopedia.* Software published by Eschalon Development Inc.

"Blessed are the poor in spirit, for theirs is the kingdom of heaven."
Truly blessed is the person who discovers his total inadequacy and unworthiness and who puts his full trust in God. With this total surrender, he can live in obedience as a citizen in the kingdom of heaven.

"Blessed are those who mourn, for they will be comforted."
Truly blessed is the person whose heart gets broken as she sees the suffering in the world and her own sinfulness. Through that sorrow, she will experience the inner joy that comes from God.

"Blessed are the meek, for they will inherit the earth."
Truly blessed is the person who is able to control his instincts and motives and place himself under the sovereignty of God. This person is humble enough to know his inadequacy and unworthiness, and in this humility gains the respect of people.

"Blessed are those who hunger and thirst for righteousness, for they will be filled."
Truly blessed is the person who yearns and longs for righteousness like she thirsts for water and hungers for food after a long day of fasting. This person will be deeply and totally satisfied.

"Blessed are the merciful, for they will be shown mercy."
Truly blessed is the person who gets involved in people's lives as she stands in their shoes and sees their needs through their eyes. This person will discover how to treat others with mercy, just as God treated her with even greater mercy through Christ.

"Blessed are the pure in heart, for they will see God."
Truly blessed is the person who has pure and clean motives, for his inner eyes will be opened to see God.

"Blessed are the peacemakers, for they will be called sons of God."
Truly blessed is the person who connects people together and helps them resolve their conflicts, because that is what God does.

"Blessed are those who are persecuted because of righteousness, for theirs is the kingdom of heaven. Blessed are you when people insult you, persecute you and falsely say all kinds of evil against you because of me. Rejoice and be glad, because great is your reward in heaven, for in the

same way they persecuted the prophets who were before you."
  Truly blessed is the person who is willing to speak out for righteousness and against injustice and who suffers for it. Truly blessed is the person who suffers because he loves Jesus and is living the cross as a lifestyle. This person should rejoice, for he will be rewarded with everlasting life with God and will blaze a trail for others to follow.

  I encourage you, my friend, to memorize this whole sermon and to let it permeate your thinking and your life. People memorize poems or portions of religious books that are far longer than the Sermon on the Mount. It is about 100 verses long, and it can impact you beyond your dreams and expectations.

REFLECTION AND DISCUSSION QUESTIONS

1. If you were the professor facing Mr. Didaat, what would you have said and done?
2. What is your understanding of the purposes of the law?
3. There is a minimal law that is required of every person who lives in a certain society, and there is a maximum law that shows us the absolute demands of God. How does the maximum law help you be a good citizen by going above the minimum-required law?
4. How does the Sermon on the Mount impact how you see God and how you see yourself?
5. Please go through the Sermon on the Mount at the end of the book before going to the next chapter.

CHAPTER 7

THE GREAT

TRANSACTION:

WHAT JESUS GAVE

IF I WANT TO BUY A CAR IN A THIRD WORLD COUNTRY, I WILL NEED TO decide on the car and have my money ready. When I go to buy the car, a transaction will take place involving a give-and-take. I give the seller my check with the signed papers, and he gives me the keys and the car.

To get on the moving walkway, the straight road, a different kind of transaction needs to take place between us and Christ. It is a huge transaction with a give-and-take of cosmic proportions.

When Jesus came to earth, He came with a purpose. For 33 years, He worked on this purpose, and just before His death He announced: "It is finished." Let's take a look at what He came to accomplish.

CHRIST'S PURPOSE

One of Jesus' purposes was to fulfill the law in a way that satisfied God fully and earned the 100 percent passing grade for all who believe in Him.

Remember that Moses, in his last will and testament, told the people of Israel, just before crossing the Jordan River to Canaan: *"If you fully obey the LORD your God and carefully follow all his commands I give you today, the LORD your God will set you high above all the nations on earth. All these blessings will come upon you and accompany you if you obey the LORD your God"* (Deuteronomy 28:1–2, emphasis added).

As we know from the Bible, the people of Israel failed miserably in fulfilling this condition. The Old Testament records in detail how God punished the Israelites repeatedly for their disobedience, even bringing the Babylonians to destroy Jerusalem and take most of its inhabitants as slaves and exiles. It did not take long for the Jews to realize that they could not fulfill the conditions listed in Deuteronomy 28:1–2. With time, their theology evolved to the hope that if *every single* Jew around the world on one whole day kept the law and lived in full obedience, then the condition would be fulfilled and they would earn God's acceptance. That didn't happen. So they started hoping that if a *remnant few* would fully obey and carefully follow all the commandments of God, they would earn the 100 percent passing grade for everyone. That did not happen either.

What did happen, though, is that Jesus, as the representative of all humanity, fully obeyed and carefully followed all the commandments of God every single day, earning the 100 percent passing grade on behalf of all who believe in Him. No one else in the history of humanity was told loudly and clearly by the almighty God: *"You are my Son, whom I love; with you I am well pleased'"* (Mark 1:11).

At another time when Jesus was with three of His disciples, they heard the very voice of God the Father say this about Jesus: *"This is my Son, whom I love. Listen to him'"* (Mark 9:7).

Not only did Jesus fulfill and obey the law, He also never sinned. He was truly unique. The New Testament states clearly: *"For we do not have a high priest who is unable to sympathize with our weaknesses, but we have one* [Jesus] *who has been tempted in every way, just as we are—yet was without sin"* (Hebrews 4:15).

In the cosmic transaction that we make with Jesus, there is a give and a take. When we have an encounter with Christ, surrender ourselves to Him, and believe in Him, Jesus takes all our sins—past, present, and future—upon Himself. At the same time, He gives us His perfect righteousness that satisfies God. We get undressed from the filthy rags we are wearing (our own attempts at righteousness) and get dressed with a robe of true righteousness (Isaiah 64:6, 61:10). This righteousness was earned by Christ as He lived on our planet in perfect obedience.

As the Father looks from heaven on any one of us who have had an encounter with Christ, He does not see you and me, but He sees Jesus. When He looks at us through the lenses of Jesus, God is fully pleased with us.

This was Christ's purpose. If you accept Christ's righteousness on your behalf, when God touches you, He is touching Jesus. He sees and smells Jesus in you because you are wearing Christ's robe of righteousness, which covers you from your head to your toes. You do not need to be graded on a curve to get a passing grade with God. He sees you with a 100 percent grade because of Jesus.

Two Kinds of Righteousness

When you look at Christians, what do you see? Do you see us dressed from head to toe with the robe of Christ's righteousness, free from the filthy rags of our personal efforts to please God? What passing grade would you give us?

I am sorry to say that many of us who put our faith in Christ do not reflect the reality of what we have experienced. Perhaps we started walking by faith, then we regress to personal effort. Please forgive us for being a stumbling block to you.

I remember at a certain time in my life I tried to motivate people to follow Christ by putting a guilt trip on them. So many Christians today want to motivate you to love God through that same approach: "You need to read more of the Bible. You need to come to more church activities. You need to tell more people about Christ. You need to memorize more Bible passages." I now see that this is a wrong approach, and it leads people to legalism, a ladder mentality. When we live that way, we are not that different from the Pharisees of Jesus' time.

At another time in my life, I tried to motivate people by offering them a challenge. I've seen other Christians do this too. We tell you grand stories and challenge you to measure up. We might tell you about spiritual giants who spend so many hours in prayer or so many hours in Bible study or about others who have memorized so many verses from the Bible. It is great to be inspired by people, but if this becomes the main way to motivate people, something is wrong. This approach could discourage people and also lead to a ladder mentality. When I think of the people in my past who I tried to motivate through guilt or merely through challenges, I shudder with shame and regret. I wish I could see those people again to correct the misconceptions that I communicated to them.

At this stage in my life, I believe that the true and proper motivation is the good news of being completely forgiven. When we become aware of what God is really like, we see our sinfulness and His love, and we respond to Him with gratitude. This is the right motivation, and it can be summarized in four steps:

- Focus on God—We become aware of who God is and what He is like, mostly by looking at Jesus' time on earth.
- Repent—We see the ugliness of our sin and how it is an assault on God. We ask for His forgiveness.
- Accept His forgiveness—We hear and believe the Gospel, or the Good News of how Jesus took our sin and gave us His perfect

righteousness and cleansed us from all defilement *(najasa)*. We are free from condemnation.

- Express gratitude—When we see our unworthiness, we are overwhelmed by His love.

Some people think that the Gospel is for unbelievers only. I believe that the Gospel of complete forgiveness is for everyone, believers and unbelievers. As believers in Christ, we need to keep reminding ourselves of how God sees us, which is known as "declared righteousness." The Bible tells us that as a result of what Christ accomplished on the cross—that great transaction—we were declared righteous (Romans 5:18–19). The more we focus on that, the more our "actual righteousness"—the way we live our daily lives—will reflect the fragrance of Christ. When we believe what God says about us (declared righteousness), our relationship with Him changes. The Judge becomes our loving Father. We are no longer condemned (Romans 4:8, 8:1). If, on the other hand, we focus on our efforts to please God, we can become self-righteous and develop a critical spirit. We become more and more occupied with the treadmill of Christian activities. If we focus on our sin rather than the cross of Christ, we can fall into a cycle of repeated confessions, repentance, and performance-based spirituality. I am sad to say that many Christians have fallen into this pattern.

A Cosmic Battle

There is one more component of this great transaction that we must understand. We have an enemy who wants to interrupt the transaction. Whether we see it around us or not, we are engaged every day in a cosmic battle.

Several years ago, I wrote a book on spiritual warfare titled *The Unseen Reality*. In one chapter, I described the cosmic battle between heaven and hell. Here are a few paragraphs worth repeating:

The Devil's attributes describe him. He is the Evil One (Matthew 13:19), the Murderer (John 8:44), the Deceiver (Revelation 20:10), the Destroyer (Revelation 9:11), and the Tempter (Matthew 4:3). He conceals and twists truths, blinding the minds of people (2 Corinthians 4:3–4). He uses false teachers to deceive and confuse the believers (1 Timothy 4:1–4). He oppresses people by using or causing diseases, physical or emotional, to produce bitterness in man's heart against God, resulting in alienation.

The Devil's names shed more light on his powers and function. His names are Satan (Mark 4:1), the Devil (Luke 8:12), the Dragon, symbol of strength and power (Revelation 12:17), the Serpent, symbol of deception (Revelation 12:9), the Prince of the World (John 12:31), the Ruler of the Kingdom of the Air (Ephesians 2:2), and the God of this Age (2 Corinthians 4:4).

The crucifixion and resurrection of Christ were the turning point in history, for through the blood of Christ, the universe was reconciled with God (Colossians 1:20). In some books of the New Testament, death is synonymous with the Devil, because death was the Devil's greatest weapon. But through the cross, Christ took away the power of death (Romans 8:38). Death was the last enemy (1 Corinthians 15:26; Revelation 20:14) whose power was broken (2 Timothy 1:10). Death was the payment for sin, but when Jesus made the payment for us, death's power was broken at its roots. Once sin was overcome, death became like a poisonous wasp that loses its sting. Although our physical bodies still die, we no longer need to fear death because of the eternal life we have in Christ.

Before Christ, death was terrifying. No one knew exactly what happened after death. Hades, the place of the dead, was only a vague concept in the Old Testament era. But when Christ was crucified and resurrected, death became an open door to eternal life with God. In this way, Christ disarmed the Devil (Colossians 2:15). It is no wonder that the Devil's main strategy is deception, because when we know the truth and follow it, the Devil becomes powerless. His purpose is still the same—spiritual destruction of all humanity by keeping us in spiritual darkness and alienation from God. However, the Devil has lost his greatest power, so he compensates through deception.

World War II's D-Day, June 6, 1944, guaranteed victory for the Allies when their invasion of Normandy was successful. But it did not mean that all the battles stopped. Several battles continued for weeks and even months. The bullets were real, and the bloodshed continued. The same is true in our spiritual warfare. The day Jesus rose from the dead was D-Day. On that day, the war was won, and the Devil was defeated. His strongest weapons were destroyed, yet the battle continues. One day, on the Day of Judgment, the battles will cease and the Devil will be completely crushed.

We are going to be involved in warfare with this Enemy. How successful we are will be determined by how we see him. Do we face our daily spiritual battles knowing that the Enemy has been defeated and that victory is ours through Christ? Or do we continue to wrestle with him day after day, fighting for our very lives, not knowing what the outcome will be?

In this chapter, we have focused primarily on one side of the transaction—what Christ gave. In the next chapter, we will get into what Christ took away. As we consider this cosmic transaction, picture Christ successfully climbing the descending escalator on behalf of those who believe in Him, pulling them off, and placing them on the moving walkway.

REFLECTION AND DISCUSSION QUESTIONS

1. In this cosmic transaction, what did Jesus give? Why was He able to do it?
2. Do you see the Devil as a defeated enemy (though he still fights tenaciously) or as someone who has power over you?
3. What did you learn from this chapter about our enemy, the Devil?
4. What did Christ's death and resurrection do to the Devil?

CHAPTER 8

THE TRANSACTION

COMPLETED:

WHAT JESUS TOOK

AS WE SAW IN THE PREVIOUS CHAPTER, THE HUGE COSMIC TRANSACTION between human beings and Jesus involves a give-and-take. To those who believe in Him, Jesus gives His perfect righteousness, the 100 percent passing grade. He also gives an assurance of victory over the Devil and the promise of eternal life. He gives us the privilege of being placed on the moving walkway and living in an atmosphere of grace, rather than living in shackles on the descending escalator.

So what is the take involved in the transaction? What does Jesus take from us? Simply put, *He takes our sin.* He was accused of every sin we ever committed or ever will commit, and He was declared guilty. He was crucified outside the city of Jerusalem because the Jews did not want Him to defile their holy city. Paul wrote in Galatians 3:13, *"Christ redeemed us from the curse of the law by becoming a curse for us, for it is written: 'Cursed is everyone who is hung on a tree.'"* (Crosses were made from trees.) He was stripped almost completely naked to cover our nakedness and shame. Jesus took upon Himself our shame, defilement *(najasa)*, and depravity.

More than 700 years before the time of Christ, the prophet Isaiah prophesied in amazing detail about the life of Christ and His suffering. He described what would happen to Christ, more than 700 years later, like this:

"He was looked down on and passed over, a man who suffered, who knew pain firsthand. . . . But the fact is, it was our pains he carried—our disfigurements, all the things wrong with us. We thought he brought it on himself, that God was punishing him for his own failures.

But it was our sins that did that to him, that ripped and tore and crushed him—our sins! He took the punishment, and that made us whole.

Through his bruises we get healed. We're all like sheep who've wandered off and gotten lost. We've all done our own thing, gone our own way. And GOD has piled all our sins, everything we've done wrong, on him, on him. He was beaten, he was tortured, but he didn't say a word. Like a lamb taken to be slaughtered and like a sheep being sheared, he took it all in silence. Justice miscarried, and he was led off—and did anyone really know what was happening? He died without a thought for his own welfare, beaten bloody for the sins of my people.

They buried him with the wicked, threw him in a grave with a rich man. Even though he'd never hurt a soul or said one word that wasn't true. Still, it's what GOD had in mind all along, to crush him with pain. The plan was that he give himself as an offering for sin so that he'd see life come from it—life, life, and more life. And GOD's plan will deeply prosper through him. Out of that terrible travail of soul, he'll see that it's worth it and be glad he did it. Through what he experienced, my righteous one, my servant, will make many 'righteous ones,' as he himself carries the burden of their sins. Therefore I'll reward him extravagantly—the best of everything, the highest honors—Because he looked death in the face and didn't flinch, because he embraced the company of the lowest. He took on his own shoulders the sin of the many, he took up the cause of all the black sheep" (Isaiah 53:3–12, *The Message*).

To completely understand what Jesus took from us, we must look at the cross and what it meant.

The Importance of the Cross

In 2004, the year the movie *The Passion of the Christ* was released, I saw three TV interviews with Mel Gibson, the movie's director. In one, Gibson was asked about the brutality of the movie. He responded by saying something like this: "Well, I wanted to push people off the edge." When I heard his response, I wondered what he meant. A couple of weeks later, after watching the movie for the third time, I was pushed off the edge.

A year later, I was visiting with a Muslim doctor who had seen the movie, and I asked him what he thought of it. His response made sense from a human perspective. He told me that he could not understand why Jesus persisted in carrying the cross to the very end if He knew that they were going to kill him anyway. Why didn't He give up and refuse to cooperate?

In the previous chapter, we talked about how death was the Devil's strongest weapon. Before the death and the resurrection of Christ, death was a terrifying experience, and for Muslims, it continues to be. There are many books written by Muslims on the dying process and on the tortures of the grave. If Jesus gave up on His way to the cross without persevering to the very end, the Devil would have won. He would still be able to torment us with the fear of death.

In *The Passion of the Christ,* the Devil is presented in a clever way and with a face that is always defiant. In the flashbacks, the Devil's expression looks as if he is saying to Jesus: "I am going to get you." During the lashing and the torture of Jesus by the Roman soldiers, the Devil's face communicates, "I got you." At the very end of the movie, when Christ dies on the cross, there is a final scene of the Devil. He is at the bottom of a very deep pit, his face no longer defiant but defeated. D-Day was declared. Victory was won as Jesus completed the transaction.

During the torture and the journey to the cross, Jesus was determined to go all the way. He had a purpose, and He wanted to accomplish it. He refused to be a victim or to give up. He did not say, "I am finished." Instead, He said, "*It* is finished" when the transaction was completed.

THREE MEANINGS OF THE CROSS

The cross is central to understanding God's character. The cross was not only a means of execution used to kill Jesus; it was how He lived His life—a lifestyle of sacrifice. He gave up heaven to come to our planet. He put our welfare before His own. This is living the cross as a lifestyle. The apostle Paul exhorted followers of Christ in Philippi to live this way as well:

"Do nothing out of selfish ambition or vain conceit, but in humility consider others better than yourselves. Each of you should look not only to your own interests, but also to the interests of others" (Philippians 2:3–4).

These verses describe a lifestyle of humility, selflessness, and concern for the welfare of others. When we look at Jesus, we see the prime example of this.

It is not uncommon for those who live the cross as a lifestyle to be taken advantage of by selfish people. The cross comes at a cost. Jesus paid this high price even though He knew many people would not accept the gift He purchased with His life. Before the crucifixion, He told the following story, which we read in Luke chapter 17:

"Now on his way to Jerusalem, Jesus traveled along the border between Samaria and Galilee. As he was going into a village, ten men who had leprosy met him. They stood at a distance and called out in a loud voice, 'Jesus, Master, have pity on us!'" (verses 11–12).

In those days the lepers were considered unclean, and they were supposed to keep away from other people so they would not defile and infect them. These 10 lepers must have heard about the kindness and selflessness of Jesus and His power to heal, so they dared to approach Him and ask Him for help.

"When he saw them, he said, 'Go, show yourselves to the priests.' And as they went, they were cleansed. One of them, when he saw he was healed, came back, praising God in a loud voice. He threw himself at Jesus' feet and thanked him—and he was a Samaritan. Jesus asked, 'Were not all ten cleansed? Where are the other nine?'" (verses 14–17).

The lack of gratitude shown by the nine who did not return exemplifies the human heart. We take advantage of God. We want Him to heal us, to bless us, to protect us from harm, to take care of our families, and to provide for us. When He does all of these things, many of us forget even to thank Him. We might even treat Him as if He does not exist.

Jesus was tortured and crucified—a high cost for living the cross as a lifestyle. The two hours of His suffering we see in *The Passion of the Christ* is a *brief* account of what happened in about 10 hours of pain and humiliation. He experienced unimaginable torture to secure for us victory over the Devil and freedom from the fear of death. His purpose was to unshackle us from living every day on a descending escalator, terrified of death and without hope.

Jesus lived the cross as a *lifestyle,* and as a result He experienced the cross as a *cost.* And because He didn't quit but completed the transaction, He experienced the cross as *victory and power.*

The cross was, perhaps, the most cruel execution instrument ever used. Hangings, firing squads, decapitations, lethal injections, and the electric chair all look tame in comparison. Yet today the cross has new meaning because of the victory that Jesus achieved as He completed the transaction. Can you imagine ladies today wearing a little electric chair hanging on a golden chain around their necks? Can you imagine a church building with a beautiful guillotine on the top? Because of what Jesus did, the cross today is a symbol of victory rather than a horrific symbol of death.

In a passage in the book of Philippians, the apostle Paul describes the three aspects of the cross: the cross as lifestyle, the cross as a cost, and the cross as victory and power.

"Think of yourselves the way Christ Jesus thought of himself. He had equal status with God but didn't think so much of himself that he had to cling to the advantages of that status no matter what. Not at all. When

the time came, he set aside the privileges of deity and took on the status of a slave, became human! Having become human, he stayed human. [The cross as lifestyle.] *It was an incredibly humbling process. He didn't claim special privileges. Instead, he lived a selfless, obedient life and then died a selfless, obedient death—and the worst kind of death at that: a crucifixion.* [The cross as a cost.] *Because of that obedience, God lifted him high and honored him far beyond anyone or anything, ever, so that all created beings in heaven and on earth—even those long ago dead and buried—will bow in worship before this Jesus Christ, and call out in praise that he is the Master of all, to the glorious honor of God the Father"* [The cross as victory and power.] (Philippians 2:5–11, *The Message*).

PUSHED OFF THE EDGE

After watching *The Passion of the Christ* for the third time, I began thinking more about what Mel Gibson said in the interview—that he wanted to push people off the edge. Then, as I was reading the Bible, I came across Psalm 22. This psalm was written by David, who was king of Israel from B.C. 1055 to B.C. 1015. Before he became king, a man named Saul was king. King Saul was jealous of David and wanted to kill him. In the meantime, God was preparing David to become king.

During this time, when he was running for his life from King Saul, David wrote Psalm 22, which describes the agony he must have felt.

It seems that Jesus was meditating on the words of this particular psalm during the crucifixion and in the hours and days that preceded it. As He was on the cross, He said very few words, but one of the sentences He did say was a quotation from this psalm: "My God, my God, why have you forsaken me?" Matthew 27:46 records exactly what Jesus said on the cross as He quoted Psalm 22:1 in Aramaic: *"Eloi, Eloi, lama sabachthani?"* ("My God, my God, why have you abandoned me?")

As I meditated on Psalm 22, I thought about how David felt abandoned, even though, in reality, God was preparing him to be king. This must have been how Jesus felt too. The sin that He carried upon Himself on our behalf made him stink with shame, guilt, and defilement—so much so that God the Father turned His face away in disgust and fully abandoned Jesus. Why did Jesus do that? Because He wanted to ensure victory for you and for me and to place us on the moving walkway.

As I thought of that, a mental picture came to mind. God put Jesus on one side of the scale and put me on the other side. Then, amazingly, He favored me *at the cost of abandoning Jesus.* As I came to this deep realization, I was so overcome with the love of God that I wept. Then I realized what it meant to be pushed off the edge.

What about you? Has the truth of how much God loves you—of the price He paid for you—sunk in? Have you been pushed off the edge?

Reflection and Discussion Questions

1. What movies have you seen about Jesus Christ? How did they impact you?
2. Have you had any dreams or visions of Jesus? How did they impact you?
3. Describe the "cosmic transaction" that took place between Christ and us. Why was it important?
4. Have you ever been "pushed off the edge" by the deep realization of how much God loves you?

CHAPTER 9

A New Beginning

During His visit to our planet, Christ performed many miracles. Perhaps among the most amazing was His healing of lepers. Leprosy at that time was almost like AIDS today, and in some ways it was worse. With no hope for healing, lepers lived in communes away from other people so that they would not defile and infect the society. It is amazing not just that Jesus healed the lepers, but *how* He did it. He touched them, but instead of being defiled or infected, He healed them. Similarly, the blind had no hope for healing; there was no eye surgery in those days. Christ healed even those who were born blind. He also raised people from the dead. One man was raised four days after his death, when he was rotting in the grave. But His greatest miracle of all, the one He continues to do, was re-creating human beings—creating them anew.

An older, respected Jewish religious teacher, leader, and politician named Nicodemus came to Jesus one night after being impressed by what he heard about Christ. We read about this encounter in John 3:2–4:

"Rabbi, [teacher], *we know you are a teacher who has come from God. For no one could perform the miraculous signs you are doing if God were not with him.' In reply Jesus declared, 'I tell you the truth, no one can see the kingdom of God unless he is born again.'"*

The religious leader was confused by Jesus' response, so he asked:

"'How can a man be born when he is old? Surely he cannot enter a second time into his mother's womb to be born!'"

Jesus helped Nicodemus understand that there are two kinds of births. The first is physical and happens when a baby is born of its mother. The second, a miraculous, spiritual kind of birth, happens when a person is born of God. Jesus went on to explain to Nicodemus that God loved people so much that He provided a plan for them: If they believed in Christ, they would experience the miracle of miracles and be born again. This discussion with Nicodemus shows us that salvation *(najat)* is not about working hard to climb the descending escalator. Rather, it comes when we are miraculously placed on the moving walkway, the straight road. Being created anew is like being transformed from a caterpillar to a butterfly. The caterpillar that built a cocoon around itself and later transforms into a butterfly still has the same DNA, yet the difference between the two is huge. The caterpillar crawls, while the beautiful butterfly soars. Being born again means being transformed from one condition to another.

Before the Transformation

Apart from God, natural mankind has several characteristics. What are these? What do we exchange in the great transaction we make with Jesus?

1. Defilement (najasa) and depravity.

We see an example of defilement or uncleanliness when the Old Testament law describes a woman having her period.

"*. . . anyone who touches her will be unclean till evening. Anything she lies on during her period will be unclean, and anything she sits on will be unclean. Whoever touches her bed must wash his clothes and bathe with water, and he will be unclean till evening*" (Leviticus 15:19–21).

A good Muslim friend of mine told me how sad he feels for his wife. When she gets her monthly period during the month of Ramadan, she continues to fast like everyone else in the family, but deep in her heart she knows that her fasting does not count because she is unclean. So when the month of Ramadan is over and everybody is celebrating with wonderful food and sweets, this woman is fasting alone to compensate for the days that did not count.

Jesus contrasted defilement *(najasa)* with inner cleanliness *(tahara)* like this:

"'*What comes out of a man is what makes him "unclean." For from within, out of men's hearts, come evil thoughts, sexual immorality, theft, murder, adultery, greed, malice, deceit, lewdness, envy, slander, arrogance and folly. All these evils come from inside and make a man "unclean"'*" (Mark 7:20–23).

What is the difference between defilement and depravity? In our everyday language, we tend to think of defilement as being externally unclean. So when people practice the ceremonial washings, they become clean from external defilement. Depravity is a bigger issue and has to do with inner *najasa* or uncleanliness. Depravity cannot be taken care of by ceremonial washings. It takes far more than that. It requires a blood sacrifice *(kaffara)*. Consider this illustration.

Suppose that on a hot day I exercise and come back home sweating and thirsty. My son wants to serve me by giving me a glass of water to drink. After receiving the glass of water, I see a very small piece of paper floating on the surface. It is easy for me to get rid of that little piece of paper and then drink the water. But suppose my son, before giving me the glass of water, places a few drops of black ink into the glass. Will I drink this filthy water? Of course not. Defilement is like that little piece of paper floating on the surface of the water. Depravity is like the ink drops that infiltrate the whole glass of water and make it filthy.

When we come before the almighty God, let us remember that the barrier separating us from Him is not our external defilement but, more important, our inner depravity.

2. Shame ('aar).

Shame is central in the Arab world. In Jordan, up until late in the 20th century, if a man killed his sister because she had committed adultery, he was sentenced to only one year of imprisonment. (If that Jordanian man murdered a person for other reasons, the punishment could be imprisonment for life.) The message is that committing adultery brings shame to the family, and it needs to be "wiped out" through the spilling of blood. Cleaning and wiping out shame is essential, not only in the Arab world but also in other religions and cultures.

Sin brings about not only guilt but also shame. Sometimes the sense of shame is even stronger than the guilt. A student may experience some guilt if she cheats on a school exam. If she gets caught cheating, the sense of shame is even more painful.

Humans are in a condition of shame when they stand before God. Adam, after his sin, hid and did not want to be in the presence of God. Yet before his sin, he enjoyed deep intimacy with God and looked forward to being in His presence. After he disobeyed God, he started avoiding God because of his shame (Genesis 3:8).

Cain, one of the sons of Adam, killed his brother Abel and lived with the consequences. He lived with shame and guilt and was described in the Bible as a restless wanderer, hidden from the presence of God. Shame can eat away at you until it destroys your life.

3. Fear of the demonic and of dying.

Earlier I talked about how the Devil is intent on destroying humans. The Devil's weapons, such as fear of demons and of being demon possessed, are terrifying.

The dying process is also terrifying for every human who does not know what is on the "other side." Can you imagine flying out of your local airport and not knowing where you were flying to?

4. Condemnation by God.

In Chapter 5, we talked about the "book" being opened on the Day of Judgment that contains a record of every sin a person has ever committed. This book is a witness against that person, who stands guilty before God. I used an illustration showing that even the purest, most zealous person will have a huge book with a minimum of 60,000 sins to account for. No matter how well we think we are doing at climbing the descending escalator, we are condemned by the holy God who has absolute standards. He will accept nothing less than a 100 percent passing grade.

AFTER THE TRANSFORMATION

We've seen what we bring to the exchange. What does Jesus give us as part of this transaction?

Jesus said to His disciples: *"'I no longer call you servants* (slaves/ *'abeed), because a servant does not know his master's business. Instead, I have called you friends, for everything that I learned from my Father I have made known to you'"* (John 15:15).

In the Gospel of John, we have a description of Jesus and what happens to those who surrender their lives to Him. *"He came to that which was his own* [the Jewish people], *but his own did not receive him. Yet to all who received him, to those who believed in his name, he gave the right to become children of God—children born not of natural descent, nor of human decision or a husband's will, but born of God"* (John 1:11–13).

All who believe in Christ and surrender their lives to Him will move:
- From defilement *(najasa)* and depravity to *cleanliness*—complete cleanliness on the inside.
- From shame and slavery to sin to a place of *honor* in God's kingdom.
- From fear of death to *hope and certainty* about eternal life with God.
- From bondage to the Devil and his demons to *deliverance* and *freedom from fear.*
- From being condemned by God as guilty, deserving to go to hell, to being declared *not guilty* (*"Therefore, there is now no condemnation for those who are in Christ Jesus"*—Romans 8:1).
- From being a restless wanderer, hidden from the presence of God, to being accepted by God and living with a *clear conscience.*
- From spiritual blindness to having the *eyes of the heart opened*—

seeing Jesus for who He really is.
- From being a servant/slave of God (*'abd*) to being *born of God* (born again) and becoming a *child of God*.

Many years ago, I saw an interesting diagram in the book *The Ultimate Intention* by DeVern Fromke. I have modified the diagram to show more clearly what happens when a person gets transformed from being a servant/slave of God to becoming a child of God.

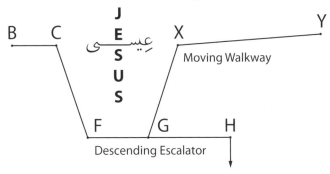

God designed earth as the place to carry out His plan, so He created humans in His own image (Point B). He wanted them to grow and become like His beloved Son, Jesus, and to move toward Point Y on the moving walkway. But these humans became self-centered and declared their independence from their Creator. They treated Him with contempt, and some defied Him. They dropped down and lived at a level God never intended for them (Point F) and began to climb a descending escalator. If these people do not repent and respond to God, He will declare them guilty on the Day of Judgment (Point H).

There is a solution, however, for those living a hopeless life on the descending escalator. Christ made the ultimate transaction with humans who recognize Him for who He is and respond to Him. He lifts these people from the descending escalator (Line FH) and places them on the moving walkway (Line XY). He gave them His perfect righteousness and purity, taking their sin upon Himself. He gets them unshackled and through the Holy Spirit equips them with tremendous potential for growth.

"For if, when we were God's enemies [Line FH], *we were reconciled to him through the death of his Son, how much more, having been reconciled* [Line GX], *shall we be saved through his life* [moving forward on the moving walkway]*!"* (Romans 5:10).

My friend, where are you on the diagram? Are you on Line XY, moving forward on the moving walkway? Or are you on Line FH, trying to climb the descending escalator day in and day out? Or are you stuck on Point G, ready to make a change but not knowing what to do? Maybe you're even stuck at Point X, like a spiritual baby who is sick and not growing.

You might think that you are somewhere between Points X and G. While human gestation takes nine months and growth takes a lifetime, spiritual birth takes only minutes. You cannot be somewhere between X and G. You are either at one point or the other.

If you answer that you are on Line XY, how do you know that? What did you do to get there? If, on the other hand, you answered that you are on Line FH, what do you need to do to move from G to X?

Please do not hurry in this evaluation. This question could well be the most important of your life.

REFLECTION AND DISCUSSION QUESTIONS
1. How would you describe in detail the "first condition"—what humans are like before they are transformed by Jesus?
2. How would you describe in detail the "second condition"—what they are like after the transformation?
3. How do the first and second conditions fit with the metaphors of the descending escalator and the moving walkway?
4. With a pencil, if possible, mark exactly where you are on the diagram. How do you know that you are on that particular spot?

CHAPTER 10

CONNECTING

WITH GOD

IF YOU HAVE SPENT ANY PART OF YOUR LIFE IN A THIRD WORLD COUNTRY, you know what it is like to listen to shortwave radio. It is a challenge, to say the least. Unlike AM or FM bands, the wavelength has to be exact to hear what is being said.

Any good connection requires a speaker, a listener, and the right wavelength. If I listen intently and have the right wavelength but it's at a time when there is no broadcast, it is useless. If there is a speaker and I have the right wavelength yet I am distracted and not really listening, the connection is not made. If there is a speaker and I really want to listen but I do not have the right wavelength, then I will not receive the message. A connection with God requires a speaker (God), a willing listener who will respond, and the right wavelength.

God spoke throughout history, but He spoke uniquely through Christ. *"In the past God spoke to our forefathers through the prophets at many times and in various ways, but in these last days* he has spoken to us by his Son, *whom he appointed heir of all things, and through whom he made the universe. The Son is the radiance of God's glory and the* exact representation of his being, *sustaining all things by his powerful word. After he had provided purification for sins, he sat down at the right hand of the Majesty in heaven"* (Hebrews 1:1–3, emphasis added).

The unknowable God made Himself known to us through Christ. If you want to know what God is like, take a good look at Jesus. A great deal of what can be known about God is revealed through Christ (Colossians 1:15). God has spoken through Christ, His Word *(Kalimatuhu)*. His life and words are presented in the Bible—the right wavelength. The only missing piece for the connection to be made is for you and me, my friend, to listen and respond. What does that involve? To answer this question, I will use a story that Jesus told during His time on earth.

The Story of the Father[1]

Jesus often was surrounded by crowds, including the rejects of society: tax collectors, prostitutes, and "sinners." Jewish tax collectors were perceived as traitors because they collected money from the Jews for the Roman occupiers. Furthermore, they made a great deal of money in the process and abused their own people. They were especially hated by those who made up the religious establishment. For some reason, these "rejects" were drawn to Jesus in spite of His perfect purity and sinlessness. Similarly, prostitutes and sinners who did not have time or the desire to observe the letter of the law were also looked down on by the religious establishment. Yet they too were drawn to Jesus.

"Now the tax collectors and 'sinners' were all gathering around to hear him. But the Pharisees and the teachers of the law muttered, 'This man welcomes sinners and eats with them'" (Luke 15:1–2).

Another group within the crowd were the Pharisees. Their significance came from the fact that they possessed great power. They were religious legalists who tried to follow the law *(sharia)* to the letter and imposed their understanding of righteousness on everyone else. They hated Jesus for many reasons, including the way He treated the "lost" *(daalleen)*, giving them honor and dignity. The Pharisees wanted Him to treat these people with contempt. Instead, He welcomed repentant sinners and called the religious leaders hypocrites.

With this mixed audience before Him, Jesus told three stories, recorded in Luke 15. I will focus on His third story, which is actually a story about God. The Bible text is in italics, and my comments are in brackets.

"There was a man who had two sons. [Remember, this story is an allegory about God and the two types of "children" He has.] *The younger one said to his father, 'Father, give me my share of the estate.' So he divided his property between them.* [The younger son represents the sinners and rejects. As an Arab who grew up in the Middle East, three things surprise me about this request. First, how could a son approach his father and ask for his share of the inheritance while the father was still alive? This is *shameful*. In those days, people did not keep their money in the bank. The money was mostly in land, property, and livestock. For the father to give this son his share of the inheritance, he had to sell something, and

---

1 I have learned a great deal from my friend Kenneth Bailey, who has helped me see the life of Christ in an Eastern context rather than with Western filters. Jesus was neither a European nor a Westerner. He grew up in my part of the world, the Middle East. I am very much indebted to Dr. Bailey for the ideas in this chapter. For more information about his books, see his website: www.shenango.org/kbbooking.htm.

probably at a devalued price. As the news spread in the town, can you imagine the sense of indignation people must have felt toward this ungrateful, greedy, disrespectful, and shameful son? The second thing that surprises me is the silence of the older brother. He should have tried to persuade this younger brother to come to his senses and ask the forgiveness of their father. The older brother should have pleaded with his father to forgive this foolish, ungrateful son and to be patient with him. He should have been a peacemaker; instead, he was silent. His silence is very loud in this culture. The third and most surprising thing is that the father actually divided his property between them and gave the younger son his inheritance. The father's tolerance and patience were amazing.]

"Not long after that, the younger son got together all he had, set off for a distant country and there squandered his wealth in wild living." [We do not know exactly how the wealth was spent, but his older brother assumed that he spent the money on prostitutes. At any rate, it would not take long for a young man in the city to waste away his cash.]

"After he had spent everything, there was a severe famine in that whole country, and he began to be in need. So he went and hired himself out to a citizen of that country, who sent him to his fields to feed pigs. He longed to fill his stomach with the pods that the pigs were eating, but no one gave him anything." [This son became totally bankrupt. He had no money, no friends, no family, and no honor, and he was forced to work for a defiled Gentile. Can you imagine a Jew, who does not eat pork (*haram* food), having to feed pigs? Even worse, he longed to eat what the pigs ate. His shame and emptiness must have been horrible.]

"When he came to his senses, he said, 'How many of my father's hired men have food to spare, and here I am starving to death! I will set out and go back to my father and say to him: "Father, I have sinned against heaven and against you. I am no longer worthy to be called your son; make me like one of your hired men."' So he got up and went to his father." [When people come to the end of themselves and see the futility of their own efforts, they begin to hear the voice of God through their consciences. This younger son remembered his father and had, to some extent, a correct understanding of his character. He could count on his mercy. At least his father treated his servants better than the young man was being treated. When he decided to go back home, he knew it would not be easy. Deep in his heart, he believed that his father would be fair but also merciful. He knew that his older brother would be angry and not merciful. He knew how people would treat him because of the great shame he brought to his extended family and the whole town. In spite

of all these obstacles, he decided to go back home.]

"But while he was still a long way off, his father saw him and was filled with compassion for him; he ran to his son, threw his arms around him and kissed him." [It seems that the father was watching for this son, knowing that sooner or later his lost son would come back. Even if he was broken and unworthy, the father was ready to forgive him and accept him back. When he saw his son from a distance, the father knew what kind of "reception" this son would receive from the town bullies. So the father ran to his son. How can a man run when he is wearing a long robe down to his ankles? The only way I know is for this dignified older man to lift up his robe, exposing his underwear as he ran to meet his son. He did this even though nakedness was shameful in his culture, as it continues to be in the Middle East. The town's people, who must have been ready to beat up this disrespectful, greedy son, must have snickered at this older man who ran to love and protect his shameful son. What an amazing father! He risked his own reputation to protect his unworthy son. In this story, the father represents Jesus, with the cross as His core value and His lifestyle. Jesus was describing His own attitude toward sinners and to those who knew that they were lost and unworthy.]

"The son said to him, 'Father, I have sinned against heaven and against you. I am no longer worthy to be called your son.'" [It seems the son had memorized a confession for his father, but the father interrupted him and did not let him finish.]

"The father said to his servants, 'Quick! Bring the best robe and put it on him. Put a ring on his finger and sandals on his feet. Bring the fattened calf and kill it. Let's have a feast and celebrate. For this son of mine was dead and is alive again; he was lost and is found.' So they began to celebrate." [What a description of what God is like! God is the righteous judge, who at the same time is merciful and compassionate. He acknowledges us in our shameful condition, just as this father identified his shameful child by saying, *"this son of mine."* We saw this in Jesus, who accepted those who came to Him with humility and a sense of unworthiness. Because the father was willing to forgive his son and treat him with dignity and honor, the people of the town, including the leaders, were willing to do the same. But what about the older brother?]

"Meanwhile, the older son was in the field. When he came near the house, he heard music and dancing. So he called one of the servants and asked him what was going on. 'Your brother has come,' he replied, 'and your father has killed the fattened calf because he has him back safe and sound.' The older brother became angry and refused to go in." [We now

see the heart of stone this older brother had for his younger brother. What were his motivations? They could have been jealousy and anger, toward not only his brother but also his father. This older brother must have been fed up with a life of legalism, always trying to please his father by observing the letter of the law but without having a heart for the family. The older son represents the Pharisees and the religious leaders who were angry with Jesus because He welcomed the "lost" and forgave them. As Jesus talked, He was actually telling His own story about the two types of people standing right there.]

"So his father went out and pleaded with him." [This is another example of the cross as a lifestyle. The older son should have gone up to the house and welcomed his brother. Instead, he insulted his father in front of all the guests by refusing to come into the house.]

"But he answered his father, 'Look! All these years I've been slaving for you and never disobeyed your orders. Yet you never gave me even a young goat so I could celebrate with my friends. But when this son of yours who has squandered your property with prostitutes comes home, you kill the fattened calf for him!'" [Does this sound like a ladder mentality—trying to please God by climbing the descending escalator but having no intimacy with Him? This father had actually lost two sons. The younger discovered that he was lost and repented; the other did not have a clue that he was equally lost. What a tragedy.]

"'My son,' the father said, 'you are always with me, and everything I have is yours. But we had to celebrate and be glad, because this brother of yours was dead and is alive again; he was lost and is found.'" [The father tried to help this older son humanize instead of demonize his younger brother. He called him *"this brother of yours."* He wanted to remind him that they were brothers. If the people of the town forgave him and accepted him back, couldn't his own family? Through the words of the father, Jesus was telling the Pharisees and the religious leaders that the "lost" are their brothers and sisters. He also showed them why God is so merciful and forgiving to sinners.]

Is this the end of the story? I believe that if Jesus told this story after the crucifixion and the resurrection, He might have finished it by describing what happened to the father and his two sons.

The older son thought he had a living relationship with his father, but that relationship did not exist. He was driven by duty rather than love. But the younger son came to the end of himself and sensed his unworthiness. He responded to his father's love and made a life-altering connection with him.

Reread this story about the father and son, replacing yourself with the younger son and the father with God. When you come to Him, tired of climbing the ladder and at the end of your own efforts, He runs to welcome you to life on the moving walkway. He greets you with arms wide open and says, "I've been waiting for you." This is what it means to make a connection with God.

Reflection and Discussion Questions

1. How is your "connection" with God? Is there a speaker? Are you on the right wavelength? Are you listening?
2. What do you think about the story of the father and his two sons? Is this story relevant today like it was relevant at the time of Christ? How?
3. Is your attitude more like the older son or the younger son? Are you driven by duty *(fard),* trying hard to please God by climbing a descending escalator? Or have you realized your own unworthiness and would like to live on the moving walkway?
4. How could you become more like the younger son?
5. Do you long to have an encounter with God? If you do, how will the encounter take place? What practical steps are you taking to make that happen?

CHAPTER 11

UNITY IN

DIVERSITY

PERHAPS, MY MUSLIM FRIEND, YOU ARE ATTRACTED TO JESUS AND believe He was who He said. You have seen what He gave and what He took in the great transaction He made with us. Maybe you have even had an encounter with Him. Still, you may have reservations about following Him because of what you think about His other followers. Remember what I said earlier about not throwing the baby out with the bathwater. In this chapter, we'll address this important question, "Does following Christ mean becoming a carbon copy of other Christians?"

You may have believed that following Christ requires changing your name to a "Christian" name, abandoning your Muslim family, and attacking Islam. We'll see in this chapter that this is not the case. It is true, though, that some Christians assume there can be no *unity* unless there is *uniformity*.

A friend of mine I will call Abdullah is a follower of Christ from a Muslim background. For a few years, he studied at a Bible college in the United States. His new friends at the Bible college felt called by God to break every Muslim form and habit he had so that he would become just like them. From their perspective, that was how he could become a "real" Christian.

Since he was a child, Abdullah said *"Bismillah,"* which means "in the name of God," before he began eating. His father ingrained this habit into his life, and it became part of his being. His Bible college friends watched him closely before meals, and if they saw his lips moving they said, in an attempt at accountability: "You said it." He would apologize and promise never to do it again.

When God looked at that situation, it must have broken His heart to see the box mentality of His children, who believed that unity can exist only in uniformity. But I believe that the Bible teaches there is unity in diversity.

If I were to show the two following diagrams to Christians and ask them which represents a church, perhaps every one of them would point to Diagram 1.

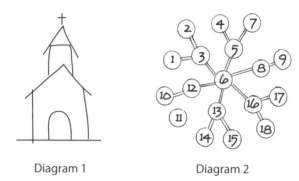

Diagram 1   Diagram 2

When people, whether Christians or Muslims, think of "church," what comes to their minds: a building, distinct architecture, a gathering on Sunday morning, singing hymns, sitting in pews, collecting the offering, and so forth? All of that they may see in Diagram 1. But what about Diagram 2? Could it represent a church as a network of people who are surrendered to Christ?

Diagram 2 shows a group of people connected with one another. Individuals such as 6 seem to be highly influential, while 11 seems to be marginal. Yet both are precious to God. Furthermore, we see in this diagram that what connects those individuals with one another are not lines but channels of relationships. These channels could be either blocked or open. Can you imagine what would happen if 6 put his trust in Christ? What would happen if 6 began to clear these relationship channels by being humble, asking for forgiveness when necessary, and reaching out to others in love like Jesus did? Can you imagine if this person refrained from self-righteous preaching at others and let his lifestyle articulate the Gospel? What if his life's mission was to live out the following two passages?

"Do not repay anyone evil for evil. Be careful to do what is right in the eyes of everybody" (Romans 12:17).

"Give thanks in all circumstances, for this is God's will for you in Christ Jesus" (1 Thessalonians 5:18).

Can you envision the church as "the people of God" and not just as a building or the meetings that happen there? What if 6, 7, and 17 began a relationship with God, became unshackled, and began growing? What would it take for them to become an *ekklesia*, which means "people of

God"?[1] Can they remain in their own environment and still be an *ekklesia*? Are they an *ekklesia* if they don't move out into something that looks like Diagram 1, but instead they share the Good News of Christ through their relationship channels? Does the Bible allow that? This question is very important, especially when we think of our Muslim brothers and sisters who have surrendered their lives to Christ in countries where proselytizing is considered nothing less than high treason.

The New Testament Church

Has the *ekklesia* (church) always looked like what we see today? How did it start, and how did it evolve over the centuries?

We read about one of the earliest examples of the *ekklesia* after the resurrection. *"Now Peter and John went up together into the temple at the hour of prayer, being the ninth hour"* (Acts 3:1). Peter and John, two disciples of Christ, continued to go to the Jewish temple, and it seems they went there at the set time of prayer. Like Muslims who pray at five set times a day, Jews also had established times for prayer. What does this say about how Peter and John perceived themselves? It seems they saw themselves as Jews who believed in Jesus.

After the resurrection of Christ and His ascension to heaven, His followers, the *ekklesia,* started being persecuted in Jerusalem. Stephen was even stoned to death. The book of Acts, chapter 8, describes it this way:

"On that day a great persecution broke out against the church at Jerusalem, and all except the apostles were scattered throughout Judea and Samaria. Those who had been scattered preached the word wherever they went" (verses 1, 4).

So far, those scattered followers of Christ preached the word only to Jews, their own people, but in Antioch a transition took place.

"Now those who had been scattered by the persecution in connection with Stephen traveled as far as Phoenicia [Lebanon], *Cyprus and Antioch* [a city by the Mediterranean, north of Syria], *telling the message only to Jews. Some of them, however, men from Cyprus and Cyrene* [Libya], *went to Antioch and began to speak to Greeks also, telling them the good news about the Lord Jesus"* (Acts 11:19–20).

---

1 The Greek word for church is *ekklesia,* meaning the "called-out people of God." The *ekklesia* is very special to God; the Bible talks about it as the family of God, the body of Christ, and the temple of the Holy Spirit. Another important Greek word that is repeated in the New Testament is *oikos,* which is usually translated as "household." The *oikos,* or household, was the social structure during the New Testament time. In the first few centuries, the *ekklesia* penetrated the social structure of the time, the *oikos.*

At this stage, the *ekklesia,* the people of God who met together in Antioch, were not only believers in Christ from a Jewish background but also those from a Gentile or non-Jewish background.

Later, when the apostle Paul carried the Gospel to Turkey and Greece, everywhere he went he started at the town synagogue. The only exception was in the city of Philippi because there was no synagogue there. Jewish worshipers and their friends went to a place near a river to learn about God. That's where Paul went in Philippi, sticking with his practice of starting with Jews. He wanted to tell them that the Messiah they had been waiting for had come and that He was the Lord Jesus Christ.

Some Jews in these cities came to faith in Christ, while others opposed the apostle Paul and persecuted his followers. In time, more and more Gentiles began believing in Christ—so much so that Paul's primary ministry shifted to the Gentiles. To the church in Ephesus, where the majority were Gentile-background believers and where he spent the longest single time of his ministry, he wrote about unity in the *ekklesia* in spite of diversity.

"Therefore, remember that formerly you who are Gentiles by birth and called 'uncircumcised' by those who call themselves 'the circumcision' (that done in the body by the hands of men)—remember that at that time you [Gentile followers of Christ] *were separate from Christ, excluded from citizenship in Israel and foreigners to the covenants of the promise, without hope and without God in the world. But now in Christ Jesus you who once were far away have been brought near through the blood of Christ. For he himself* [Jesus Christ] *is our* [believers in Christ from Jewish and Gentile backgrounds] *peace, who has made the two one and has destroyed the barrier, the dividing wall of hostility, by abolishing in his flesh the law with its commandments and regulations. His purpose was to create in himself* one new man *out of the two, thus making peace, and in this one body to reconcile both of them to God through the cross, by which he put to death their hostility. He came and preached peace to you* [Gentile believers] *who were far away and peace to those who were near* [Jewish believers]. *For through him we both have access to the Father by one Spirit. Consequently, you are no longer foreigners and aliens, but* fellow citizens *with God's people and members of God's household, built on the foundation of the apostles and prophets, with Christ Jesus himself as the chief cornerstone"* (Ephesians 2:11–20, emphasis added).

Please look carefully at the following diagram and reread this passage in Ephesians 2:11–20.

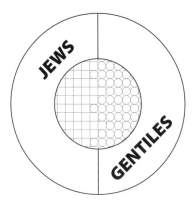

What do you observe in this diagram? The outer circle contains both Jews and Gentiles, with a wall of hostility separating them. But does that wall exist in the inner circle, the family of God? It does not. The squares, representing Jews, and the circles, representing Gentiles, live side by side, brothers and sisters within the family of God. But notice how the circles do not need to become squares to belong to the kingdom of God, and the squares do not need to become circles either. There is unity in the midst of diversity.

Implications for Today

What does the kingdom of God look like today? Must there be uniformity to achieve unity? We just looked at the Gentile/Jew controversy during Paul's time. Can we find similarities to our situation today? Certainly we can if we replace "Jews" and "Gentiles" in the diagram with "Christians" and "Muslims."

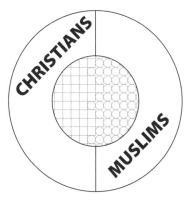

"Christians" in this diagram have 20 centuries of history. Many today are nominal Christians who do not have an intimate relationship with Christ. But those who do surrender their lives to Christ enter the kingdom, the inner circle, and maintain their "Christian" background. There are also Muslims who have surrendered to Christ and entered the kingdom, the inner circle. In the kingdom of God, there is no wall of hostility separating the "squares" from the "circles," even though we are very aware of the wall of hostility that exists outside the kingdom.

Go back to Ephesians 2:11–20 and read it again, this time replacing the word "Jew" with the word "Christian" and replacing "Gentile" with "Muslim." The first time I did this, years ago, the New Testament took on new relevance.

"Therefore, remember that formerly you [followers of Christ from a Muslim background] *who are Muslims by birth, remember that at that time you were separate from Christ. . . . But now in Christ Jesus you who once were far away have been brought near through the blood of Christ. For he himself* [Jesus Christ] *is our* [believers in Christ from Christian and Muslim backgrounds] *peace, who has made the two one and has destroyed the barrier, the dividing wall of hostility, by abolishing in his flesh the law with its commandments and regulations. His purpose was to create in himself one new man out of the two, thus making peace, and in this one body to reconcile both of them to God through the cross, by which he put to death their hostility. He came and preached peace to you* [followers of Christ from a Muslim background] *who were far away and peace to those who were near* [followers of Christ from a Christian background]. *For through him we* [followers of Christ from Christian and Muslim backgrounds] *both have access to the Father by one Spirit. Consequently, you* [followers of Christ from a Muslim background] *are no longer foreigners and aliens, but fellow citizens with God's people and members of God's household, built on the foundation of the apostles and prophets, with Christ Jesus himself as the chief cornerstone"* (Ephesians 2:11–20).

What do you think? What insights are you learning? God loves diversity. (Just look around!) He does not intend for us to all be alike. Rather, He desires to destroy the wall of hostility and reconcile all of us to Himself and to one another through the cross. There can be unity in spite of the diversity. It was true in the first century, and it's true today. Do not let this issue hold you back from giving your life to Him.

Reflection and Discussion Questions

(Some of these questions may be hard to answer on your own. Try to find a mature follower of Christ, who understands the concept of unity in diversity, to talk through these questions with you.)

1. Matthew 18:20 says, *"For where two or three come together in my [Jesus'] name, there am I with them."* In light of this verse, what are the minimum essentials for an *ekklesia?*

2. How did the apostle Paul enter the Gentile culture to reach out to them?

3. What can we learn from 1 Corinthians 9:19–23 in our contexts? Paul said, *"Though I am free and belong to no man, I make myself a slave to everyone, to win as many as possible. To the Jews I became like a Jew, to win the Jews. To those under the law I became like one under the law (though I myself am not under the law), so as to win those under the law. To those not having the law I became like one not having the law (though I am not free from God's law but am under Christ's law), so as to win those not having the law."*

4. Are there passages in the Bible that talk about remaining in context as salt and light—as an "insider"? What are these passages, and what do they teach? Look again at Diagram 2 in light of the Bible.

5. Read the Bible story of Naaman in 2 Kings 5. Naaman had a key position in the kingdom of Aram (Syria). As a result of his sickness and healing, he came to believe in the almighty God. He struggled with the issue of remaining as an insider. What insights can we learn from his story, especially verse 19?

6. First Corinthians 7 is a chapter that talks about marriage. Verses 17 through 24 talk not only about marriage, but also about slavery and issues between Jews and Gentiles. What can we learn from these verses regarding the people of God who remain in and penetrate their contexts?

CHAPTER 12

BECOMING A
CHILD OF GOD

YOU HAVE MADE IT TO CHAPTER 12! BY NOW, I HOPE MOST OF YOUR questions have been answered (though you may well have new questions also). I hope you have a very good understanding of how much God loves you, the high price He paid for you, and how much He wants you to come live with Him on the moving walkway. It may seem like a very big step to jump from the descending escalator to the moving walkway, and you may be wondering how to do it. This chapter will help you see how simple it really is.

In Chapter 9, we read a passage from the Gospel of John that describes our part in the great transaction. John wrote:

"He came to that which was his own [the Jewish people], *but his own did not receive him. Yet to all who received him, to those who believed in his name, he gave the right to become children of God—children born not of natural descent, nor of human decision or a husband's will, but born of God"* (John 1:11–13).

Who was it that became children of God? Those who *"received Him"* and *"who believed in His name."* How can we be like them? In a practical and very clear way, let's look at how a person can receive Christ and believe in Him.

This was my big question in March of 1961. I was in my last year of high school, and for the first time in my life, I came to the amazing realization that I could actually become a child of God. God wanted to take me into His family. I would no longer be a servant or slave *('abd)* but a son. I longed to belong to God's family and to be clean and forgiven. So I asked the friend who was talking to me about Christ what I should do. He showed me the metaphor of the door.

Jesus used this metaphor in Revelation 3:20, explaining that there is a door representing the only entrance to a person's life. This door does

101

not have a knob or a keyhole on the outside; instead, these are on the inside. That symbolizes the fact that Jesus does not enter anyone's life by force. He gives us the freedom to respond by either inviting Him in or by refusing to open the doors of our lives to Him.

Jesus said: *"Here I am! I stand at the door and knock. If anyone hears my voice and opens the door, I will come in and eat with him, and he with me'"* (Revelation 3:20). Jesus gives three steps in this metaphor.

STEP ONE: JESUS KNOCKING

Jesus accomplished His part of the transaction at a very high cost. He lived in daily obedience and earned the righteousness that satisfied the absolute demands of God. He earned the 100 percent passing grade and is willing to give that perfect righteousness to you and me. He was shamed to give us dignity and honor. He was defiled with our sin so that He could pay for our punishment in full, to set us free from guilt and condemnation. He delivered us from fear of death and the demonic. He was the Great Sacrifice, which the Qur'an calls *Al thabh al 'azeem* (Al-Saffat/Drawn up in ranks: Surah 37 verse 107).

With His part of the transaction complete, Jesus comes to us, individually, and knocks on the "door" of our consciences, asking us whether we will open our lives and surrender our wills to Him. He says: *"Here I am. I stand at the door and knock."*

In March 1961, Jesus could have chosen richer, more popular, or better students than me in that high school in Lebanon. What amazes me is that He came to me when I was barely making it at every level. He knocked at the "door of my life," wanting to come in. I had one of three options: postpone the decision, reject His offer, or surrender everything to Him.

On that day in March, I realized that Jesus was very serious about me. He was knocking at that very time because it was the right time. Otherwise, He wouldn't have knocked. Jesus had completed His part of the transaction, and now it was my turn.

STEP TWO: OUR RESPONSE

What does it mean to open the door of your life and surrender your will to Him? It means turning over everything to Him, trusting Him with your whole life. It means taking an honest look at how you have treated Him, either with defiance or contempt. It means admitting to Him your filth *(najasa),* shame, self-centeredness, and unworthiness and coming to Him with brokenness and repentance. It also means giving up on the idea that you can earn His acceptance by your good works. This point comes when you tire of your attempts to climb the descending escalator and you cry out to Him for help.

Because this is a critical time in your encounter with Christ, the Devil will be actively pulling you back by all possible means. He might focus on your inability to get off the descending escalator. He will remind you of your sins and how in the past you failed repeatedly to reform your life and please God. He will try to convince you that it will not be any different this time. I remember for several months I believed the lie that I had to clean up my own defilement *(najasa)* first; otherwise, Christ would not be willing to come into my life.

The Devil might try to convince you to postpone the decision, telling you that it is the wrong time. How do you know when it is the right time? If you sense that Jesus is knocking now, it means that *this* is the right time.

My friend, if you sense that Christ is knocking on the door of your heart, conscience, will, and life, do not give in to the Devil. Do not listen to him, because he is lying to you. Come to God with words of repentance, such as these:

"Almighty God, I come to you admitting my shame, filth, and sinful attitude. I have treated you with contempt. At times, I even defied you and have insisted on going my own way. Have mercy on me. I believe that Jesus died a shameful death on the cross to give me dignity and cleanse me from all my defilement. He has paid the penalty for my sins, yet I have broken Your heart in the following areas:

_____

_____

_____

On the basis of Christ's death on the cross, have mercy on me. I am opening my whole life to You now. I surrender my will to You and trust You completely for the forgiveness of my sins and the gift of eternal life. Only You can clean me from my filth. Almighty God, only You can cover my nakedness. Only You can deal with my fears and uncertainties. I am willing to do whatever You ask of me, and I want to daily trust You and obey You. Amen."

STEP THREE: ASSURANCE

Christ took the first step by knocking at the door of your life because He wants to come in. Then you took the second step by responding to

His knocking and opening your life to Him. What is the third step? Let us look again at what Jesus said:

1. *I stand at the door and knock*
2. *If anyone hears my voice and opens the door*
3. *I will come in*

The third step is that Jesus will come in. This is His promise to you. If you have done step two, certainly He will do step three. You can be sure that He entered your life through His Spirit if you have asked Him to come into your life.

ACTIONS AND FEELINGS

The basis for this assurance is not your feelings but the promise of Christ. Feelings change rapidly. After you surrender to Christ, you might *feel* relieved, happy, and forgiven, but these feelings are not the foundation for the assurance. If you lose those feelings, does that mean that Christ has left you? That is impossible. Our relationship with God is not based on feelings, but on much more. It *feels* to me that the sun revolves around the earth, but I *know* that the earth revolves around the sun.

Or consider this example. At times I might not *feel* love for my wife, but I still love her through my actions and commitment. Many times it starts with the action and the feelings follow. I remember a day in Cairo when I passed by a flower shop and thought about buying my wife some roses. As I entered the shop, I had no particular feelings of love for my wife. But as the man wrapped the roses, I imagined going back to our apartment. I decided that I would not open the door with a key but would ring the bell instead. Then I thought of how my wife would come to the door, open it, and see the beautiful roses. All of a sudden, a strong feeling of love swelled in my heart. But where did my love for my wife start that day—with the feeling or with the action?

Love includes both actions and feelings, but the actions are the foundation. Jesus described it this way: "*Whoever has my commands and obeys them, he is the one who loves me. He who loves me will be loved by my Father, and I too will love him and show myself to him*" (John 14:21). Jesus did not say: "The one who has feelings of love for me is the one who loves me." He said it is the one who *obeys* who loves Him—and obedience requires an action.

BASIS OF ASSURANCE

If it's not the feelings that assure you of Christ's presence in your life, what is it? You have assurance through two things:

1. The promise of God in His Word.

In Revelation 3:20, Christ promised that if you open your life to Him, He will come in. Did you open your life to Him? So where is He now?

After I surrendered my life to Christ, for three days I was afraid that He might leave me. I vacillated between certainty and doubt. Finally, I had the courage to talk to a mature friend about my doubts and fears. He encouraged me to read John 10 every day for the next week. When I reached verses 27 and 28, the Holy Spirit gripped my heart with deep assurance and joy. Christ said: *"'My sheep listen to my voice; I know them, and they follow me. I give them eternal life, and they shall never perish; no one can snatch them out of my hand'"* (John 10:27–28).

In these two verses, Christ assures me that He gave me eternal life, that He will never leave me, and that no one can snatch me out of His hand. Right then, I knew that I was no longer climbing the descending escalator. I knew I was on the moving walkway.

2. The witness of the Holy Spirit to your heart.

When Christ comes into your life, right away the Holy Spirit begins to talk to your spirit, telling you that you now belong to the household of God *(ahl beit Allah)*. Paul wrote on this subject in his letter to the Romans.

"Those who are led by the Spirit of God are sons of God. For you did not receive a spirit that makes you a slave again to fear, but you received the Spirit of sonship. And by him we cry, 'Abba, Father.' The Spirit himself testifies with our spirit that we are God's children" (Romans 8:14–16).

Remember, my friend, what I said about our one God who is Father, Word (Jesus/*Kalimatuhu*), and Holy Spirit (*Ruhon minhu*). God the Father is *for us,* and Jesus is *with us.* The Holy Spirit lives *in us.* He is the very Spirit of God, and when He indwells you, in a unique way God Himself actually lives in you. The Holy Spirit is God in us, leading us, convicting us of sin when we fall down on the moving walkway, and stirring us to stand back up and keep walking forward.

You may wonder what it means for the Holy Spirit to speak to your spirit. Here is an example. One of my college students was a new follower of Christ. He came from a relatively poor family. His father had died a few months earlier, and he was the eldest son and the only one in college. His mother spoiled him in many ways, such as always giving him the largest portion of meat during their meal times.

The day after he surrendered his life to Christ, we were spending time together. I asked him if he sensed that the Holy Spirit was speaking to his spirit. He told me that the previous evening when he and his family were eating, his mother put the largest portion of meat on his plate as usual. He told me that for the first time ever, he felt that his selfish behavior was wrong. So when his mother went to the kitchen, he quickly divided the meat on his plate and gave a piece to each sibling. All of a sudden, he sensed the Holy Spirit filling him and assuring him that he had become a new creation. That was when he knew for sure he was on the moving walkway.

I know a number of new followers of Christ who say the Holy Spirit convicted them about their selfishness or pride. Admitting wrongs and asking for forgiveness is another big sign of becoming a new creation.

What about you, my friend? Has Jesus knocked on the door of your heart? What will you do? If you have let Him in, do you have assurance that He is with you always? I would love to hear your answers to these questions. My e-mail address is: drjabbour@nabeeljabbour.com.

In the next part, we'll look at how we grow in our relationship with God and how we walk step-by-step on the moving walkway.

Reflection and Discussion Questions

1. Using the door metaphor to describe an encounter with Christ, explain what is Christ's responsibility and what is your responsibility.
2. Feelings are not dependable in our assurance of Christ's presence in our lives. Why not?
3. How does the Holy Spirit speak to our spirits after our encounter with Christ?
4. How can you be sure you have had an encounter with Christ and that both sides of the transaction are complete?

PART II

GROWING

CHAPTER 13

THE TWO LANDLORDS

THROUGHOUT THE NEXT SEVERAL CHAPTERS, WE WILL BE LOOKING AT the life of a spiritual newborn. Just as new babies are vulnerable and need help to grow, so do new spiritual babies—new believers in Christ.

When a baby is born at a hospital, it is usually placed with other babies in a closed, secure room that is not open to the public. Often, the nurses who handle these babies wear masks to protect the infants from germs and infections, because the first few hours and days of the baby's life are critical.

The same is true for the spiritual baby, who has just experienced new spiritual birth. In the first few hours, days, and weeks in the life of a new believer, the Devil will attack, planting seeds of doubt. The Devil plays with our minds, asking these kinds of questions: How can the short prayer you prayed make you a new creation, no more a worm but a butterfly? How can you face all the world throws at you and live victoriously? Are you suddenly going to get rid of the bad habits you have practiced for years? What about the sins you know you are going to commit? What about your worries regarding the future? How are you going to handle the possibility of being abandoned by your family and friends? Can you face that shame? What can Christ practically do to help you?

Years ago, I read an illustration that helped me understand how to deal with the Devil and his constant barrage of attacks.

Imagine that you live in an apartment owned by an evil landlord who is greedy and heartless. This landlord is well connected and knows how to manipulate the people living in his building. At the end of every month he brings your bill, telling you it must be paid right away. You plead with him to wait a week or two, and grudgingly he agrees, on the condition that you pay it back with high interest. Over time, the debt accumulates, and you find yourself enslaved to this evil man.

Then, one day, a man comes to your apartment and rings the bell.

When you open the door, you see a respectable gentleman. He introduces himself and tells you that he is the new landlord. He bought the whole building, including your apartment, and he knows exactly how much you owe. Then he really shocks you: He tells you that He has paid all your debts and that you can continue to live in this apartment the rest of your life for free, and he wants to be your friend. Then he tells you that he lives in the penthouse on the top floor of the building and if there are any problems, to let him know right away.

This illustrates our new life with Jesus. It is relatively easy for new followers of Christ to believe that our debt has been paid on the cross and we have been forgiven. It is also pretty easy to believe that we have been given the opportunity for a fresh start. But what is hard to believe is that from now on, we are living for free. We know that we believed in Christ by faith, but when it comes to daily living, instead of faith we fall back on worry and hard work.

The apostle Paul wrote to the believers in Colosse:

"So then, just as you received Christ Jesus as Lord [by faith], *continue to live in him* [by faith]" (Colossians 2:6).

How did the Colossians receive Christ? By faith of course. He is telling them to walk with Christ by faith as well.

Why is it so difficult to live by faith after opening your life to Christ? It is usually because the evil landlord returns with bills he claims you need to pay. When this happens, you have three options:

1. To start a wrestling match with this evil man, who is bigger and stronger than you.
2. To argue with him until he produces evidence of your indebtedness to him. If you let him in, he will win the arguments one after the other. Although you are free, you will find yourself enslaved again to this evil landlord.
3. To shut the door, choosing to believe what the new landlord told you. Send this evil man up to the penthouse to talk with the new landlord. Of course he will not dare go.

The Devil came even to Jesus, attempting to plant seeds of doubt in His mind. After fasting for 40 days in the wilderness, Jesus became vulnerable to temptations, so the Devil came to Him with his doubting questions. Their conversation is recorded in Matthew 4:3–4:

"'If you are the Son of God, tell these stones to become bread.' Jesus answered, 'It is written: "Man does not live on bread alone, but on every word that comes from the mouth of God."'"

The Devil repeated the attack again and again, and every time Jesus used the same approach: He shut the door in the Devil's face by affirming what the Bible says and refusing to listen to him.

You can do the same. When the evil landlord comes to you with the bills and tries to enslave you again, you can refuse to listen to him by asserting your belief in the promises of the new landlord. What follows is a list of some of the doubts the Devil will attempt to plant in your mind and the assurance you can use to refute them.

Doubts About Eternal Life

One of Christ's promises to you is this:

"I tell you the truth, whoever hears my word and believes him who sent me has eternal life and will not be condemned; he has crossed over from death to life" (John 5:24).

When you hear the Good News about Jesus and believe it, you have fulfilled the condition. As soon as you have surrendered your life to Him, you can rest assured that you have the guarantee of eternal life and that you will not be condemned. You have crossed over from the descending escalator to the moving walkway, and that is where you will stay.

Doubts Because of Abandonment Fears

The old landlord may paint a picture of your life with the new landlord as very lonely and filled with abandonment and shame. He might point out that your family and friends, who live in the same building, are tolerating the old landlord, and their lives are fine. Why choose that lonely life just so you can begin a relationship with this "unknown" landlord? What will happen to your reputation? How can you survive without family and friends?

Family and friends may turn against new believers not because of their new allegiance to Jesus, but because of their self-righteousness and criticism of others' religions and traditions. Christ usually is not offensive to people, but many times, "churchianity" is offensive because it focuses on the "wrappings."

At other times, in spite of their humility and Christlikeness, new believers are persecuted because the old landlord hates the new landlord. He wants to repossess what he has lost. There is a cost involved in following the new landlord; Christ talked about it explicitly. Yet with the cost there is a huge promise. Jesus said:

"'Everyone who has left houses or brothers or sisters or father or mother or children or fields for my sake will receive a hundred times as

much and will inherit eternal life'" (Matthew 19:29).

This is a good promise to memorize. Choose to affirm and assert your faith by believing the new landlord rather than being swayed by the old landlord.

Muslims who choose to follow Christ pay a much higher cost than I have ever paid. The sorrow on the faces of your loved ones will cut deep into your heart. You will probably miss the conversations you used to have and the intimacy you shared. This is a huge loss, especially when followers of Christ from a Christian background, who are supposed to stand with you, fail you miserably. Please remember to focus on all you have in Christ. Ask God to open your eyes so that you may see how He has already blessed you with abundance.

"Praise be to the God and Father of our Lord Jesus Christ, who has blessed us in the heavenly realms with every spiritual blessing in Christ" (Ephesians 1:3).

Doubts About Living Victoriously

The old landlord used to have power over you and could control you. How will you be sure that he doesn't get into this position again? You can send him to the new landlord, who tells you that you *". . . can do everything through him* [the new landlord] *who gives* [you] *strength"* (Philippians 4:13).

You can also stand on these promises:

"No temptation has seized you except what is common to man. And God is faithful; he will not let you be tempted beyond what you can bear. But when you are tempted, he will also provide a way out so that you can stand up under it" (1 Corinthians 10:13).

"To him who is able to keep you from falling and to present you before his glorious presence without fault and with great joy—to the only God our Savior be glory, majesty, power and authority, through Jesus Christ our Lord, before all ages, now and forevermore! Amen" (Jude 1:24–25).

"Do not gloat over me, my enemy [the old landlord]! *Though I have fallen, I will rise. Though I sit in darkness, the Lord* [the new landlord] *will be my light"* (Micah 7:8).

Doubts About Complete Forgiveness

Remember the story of the little toddler walking on the moving walkway at the airport? He fell down at times, and so will you. As soon as you fall into a certain sin—especially sin that you have struggled with in the past—the old landlord will show up. He will remind you of your past sin. He will tell you how you have offended your new landlord. The Devil will talk as if he loves the new landlord and is defending Him. Remember that the goal of the old landlord is to destroy you and enslave you through his lies, because he cannot come to the new landlord with the truth. He will make you doubt if the sins of the past have really been forgiven and whether the recent fall is forgivable too. Affirm and testify to your faith with the promises of the new landlord. Get up and start walking again on the moving walkway toward your heavenly Father.

"If we confess our sins, he [the new landlord] *is faithful and just and will forgive us our sins and purify us from all unrighteousness"* (1 John 1:9).

According to this promise, you are not only forgiven but also cleansed and purified from all your defilement *(najasa)*. You can confess your sin right away by getting up and not prolonging the process. You do not need to be in a certain place at a certain time to confess your sin. You can do it right then and there because Christ is always with you. Think of that toddler who has fallen on the moving walkway. When he sees his dad's open arms and hears him say, "It is OK, get up, come," the child stops weeping, gets up, and once again wobbles forward toward his dad.

"My dear children, I write this to you so that you will not sin. But if anybody does sin, we have one who speaks to the Father in our defense— Jesus Christ, the Righteous One. He is the atoning sacrifice for our sins, and not only for ours but also for the sins of the whole world" (1 John 2:1–2).

This passage can be illustrated like this: When you drive your car, your aim is not to have any accidents. But if you do, you have full insurance, and the payments do not increase or change because of accidents in your past. We should aim not to fall into sin, but if we do, we can be completely and repeatedly forgiven and always given a fresh start. When we are forgiven, we are justified. Justification is a big word that means "just as if we never sinned." That is how God sees you, my friend, after you confess your sins to Him and are forgiven.

Doubts About God's Love and Care

When you are lonely and do not feel warm intimacy with Jesus, the Devil wants you to get carried away with these feelings. He rushes to you, sowing seeds of doubt about the love of Christ. Does the new landlord really love you? Does He care? Does He really know what you are going through, and does He have time for you?

Affirm your faith through the promises of the new landlord:

"'Are not two sparrows [the cheapest types of birds] *sold for a penny?*

Yet not one of them will fall to the ground apart from the will of your Father. And even the very hairs of your head are all numbered. So don't be afraid; you are worth more than many sparrows'" (Matthew 10:29–31).

If God cares for the worthless sparrows, you can be sure He cares about you.

Romans 8:31–35 offers even further affirmation of God's love and care for you.

"So, what do you think? With God on our side like this, how can we lose? If God didn't hesitate to put everything on the line for us, embracing our condition and exposing himself to the worst by sending his own Son, is there anything else he wouldn't gladly and freely do for us? And who would dare tangle with God by messing with one of God's chosen [you!]? *Who would dare even to point a finger? The One who died for us—who was raised to life for us!—is in the presence of God at this very moment sticking up for us* [for you]. *Do you think anyone is going to be able to drive a wedge between us and Christ's love for us?"* (*The Message*).

This is what it is like to walk on the moving walkway by faith, believing the promises of God every day and refusing to listen to the Devil's lies. You can experience deliverance from the Devil's control as you choose to trust Christ in your daily walk.

Memorizing verses from the Bible has tremendously helped me confront my doubts. (You will learn more about this in Part III of this book.) After I have memorized them, I usually review my verses when I am driving. Sometimes my mind wanders and I can't concentrate, but at other times, I enjoy deep intimacy with God as I pray over the verses. This is my way of strengthening my faith in His promises and shutting the door in the face of the old landlord.

I encourage you to memorize at least one verse from each of the five areas presented in this chapter. Go over this chapter again and choose the verses you want to memorize. There is a page at the end of the book on which you can write the references of the verses you want to memorize in the future.

Reflection and Discussion Questions

1. Has the Devil been whispering to you and planting seeds of doubt in your mind about your faith in Christ? Has he been able to deceive you?
2. In what areas have you experienced the Devil's attacks? Have you affirmed your faith? Which passages from the Bible have helped you the most?

3. Which of the five areas of doubt covered in this chapter do you struggle with the most?
4. Have you had a "falling down" experience on the moving walkway? In what areas? What helped you get up?
5. How does the illustration of the new landlord help you in your daily living?

CHAPTER 14

STRATEGICALLY
POSITIONED

THE SYRIAN TOWN IN WHICH I GREW UP IS SURROUNDED BY MOUNTAINS.
On one side of town is a relatively small mountain known to the local
boys as the place for "battles." Every late afternoon during the summer, boys from the east side of town would "battle" boys from the west
side with small rocks and slings to see who could occupy the top of the
mountain. My father participated in these "wars" as a child, and so did
I. Perhaps this tradition continues to this day.

The few times I participated in these battles, I was on the losing side.
Boys from the east side not only occupied the top of the mountain but
also reached about 100 meters onto our side. We, the west-side boys,
were entrenched in our positions, trying desperately to move up but
having no success. The east-side boys were always the victors, and we
were the losers.

One day, a day I will never forget, while we were hiding in our little
trenches trying to dodge the rocks being hurled at us, the unimaginable
happened. A man about 30 years old emerged from our side. Because
we were only 8 to 12 years old, the man looked like a giant to us. As he
came up to us, we sensed the courage in his face and voice. Loudly, he
yelled, "Follow me." His fearlessness gave us courage and excitement,
so we started following him up the mountain. When the east-side
boys saw this "giant" coming, they were scared and began to retreat.
In less than an hour, the positions in the war changed completely. We
overpowered the east-side boys, reaching the top of the mountain and
beyond! I will never forget the feeling of victory and the sense of honor
I felt that day.

Just before he left us, the man said, "You are on the top; stay at the
top." We did just that until very late that evening, wanting to prolong
and enjoy the victory.

This story illustrates our battle with the Devil. He used to make us think that he was on the top of the mountain, threatening us with his greatest weapon, the fear of death. We were defeated, overwhelmed, and intimidated. But when Christ came, He conquered the Devil and destroyed his strongest weapon. Like that man who conquered the enemy and gave us hope, Christ conquered the Enemy and gave us victory, saying to us: "You are on the top; stay at the top."

This is the message the apostle Paul had for the Ephesians. In his letter to them, he wrote:

"But because of his great love for us, God, who is rich in mercy, made us alive with Christ even when we were dead in transgressions [in the trenches of defeat]. . . . *And God raised us up with Christ and seated us with him in the heavenly realms in Christ Jesus* [at the top of the mountain]" (Ephesians 2:4–6).

My friend, if you have surrendered your life to Christ, you are right now at the very top of the mountain—seated with Christ in the heavenly realms. You might feel very far from the top if you are discouraged or defeated because of the sins you have committed. You might be struggling with doubt and despair. But you are still on top of the mountain, not because of what you did or didn't do, but because of what *Christ* did.

Let us study briefly the letter to the Ephesians, which is divided into three main sections and describes three of the identities—and the position—we have in Christ:

First section (chapters 1, 2, and 3): Saints in Christ
Second section (chapters 4, 5, 6:1–9): Ambassadors of Christ
Third section (chapter 6:10–24): Victors in Christ

SAINTS IN CHRIST

In the first three chapters of Ephesians, Paul writes about our *position* and our *privileges* in Christ. In these chapters, and especially chapter 1, Paul is like a man trying to comfort a little boy who is crying over his lost ball. He tries to explain to this little boy that it is not worth crying over; after all, his father is a billionaire!

In Ephesians 1, Paul talks about our declared righteousness *(tabri'a),* referring to followers of Christ as "saints." According to what the New Testament teaches, what makes you a saint is not how spiritual you seem or how good you are, but *where Christ has positioned you.* If you have surrendered your life to Him, you are a saint. You are at the top of the mountain!

So much of what we think about "saints" is colored by the ladder mentality. Remember the painting I described in Chapter 4? The people climbing the ladder in the painting looked more devout the higher they got. When we hear the word "saint," certain mental pictures come to our minds—pictures of a few very "religious" individuals with a special caliber of high morals or miraculous deeds. Mother Teresa, for example, was a nun who gave her life in India to serving the untouchables and the rejects of society. She is considered a "saint" by most people because of her selflessness and her love for people. Others are recognized as "saints" after their deaths, and their tombs become shrines to which people come seeking healing and guidance. This understanding of the word "saint," however, is completely different from how the word is used in the New Testament.

Remember that when God looks at us, He sees us wrapped from head to toe with the robe of righteousness of the Lord Jesus Christ. When God the Father looks at us, He sees Jesus and declares us righteous. This is the reason we are saints.

As we go back to Ephesians 1, we read: [3]*"Praise be to the God and Father of our Lord Jesus Christ, who has blessed us in the heavenly realms with every spiritual blessing in Christ.* [He has already blessed you with every spiritual blessing. Rather than pray, "Father, bless me," it is more accurate to pray, "Father, open my eyes so that I will see how you have already blessed me and placed me at the top of the mountain."] [4]*For he chose us in him before the creation of the world to be holy and blameless in his sight.* [Can you imagine this fact? Before God created the universe, He already knew you by name. He knew your genes and designed you to grow up within a certain family, religion, and race. He knew you and chose you even before Adam was created.] *In love* [5]*he predestined us to be adopted as his sons through Jesus Christ, in accordance with his pleasure and will.* [In some societies today, adoption is not looked upon favorably, but if it is viewed accurately, it is a beautiful experience. An adopted child has all the rights and privileges that a birth child has. The apostle Paul says that we are adopted by God. Can you imagine how rich and privileged we are?] . . . [7]*In him we have redemption through his blood, the forgiveness of sins, in accordance with the riches of God's grace* [8]*that he lavished on us with all wisdom and understanding.* [The word "lavish" implies pouring out with a generous rather than stingy attitude. Grace means unmerited or undeserved favor given to us.] . . . [13]*Having believed, you were marked in him with a seal, the promised Holy Spirit,* [14]*who is a deposit guaranteeing our inheritance until the redemption of those who are God's possession—to the praise of his glory.* [When you believed in Christ, the Holy Spirit came to live within you. You became a marked person.

The indwelling of the Holy Spirit in you is a down payment guaranteeing your inheritance—eternal life with Christ.]. . . *¹⁸I pray also that the eyes of your heart may be enlightened in order that you may know the hope to which he has called you, the riches of his glorious inheritance in the saints, ¹⁹and his incomparably great power for us who believe. That power is like the working of his mighty strength, ²⁰which he exerted in Christ when he raised him from the dead and seated him at his right hand in the heavenly realms"* (Ephesians 1:3–20).

In this first section of the letter to the Ephesians, we see how God has blessed us by making us His children—the children of the King of kings and Lord of lords—His saints. He has seated us with Christ at the top of the mountain and declared us righteous.

Please stop reading and spend some time in prayer, thanking God for how He has lavished His blessings on you and has given you dignity and honor. Write down what it means to have your strategic position in Christ and your privileges. This could become a list from which to start a prayer of thanksgiving.

_____

_____

_____

AMBASSADORS OF CHRIST

In Ephesians 4, 5, and 6:1–9, Paul talks about living the victorious lifestyle and how our *actual righteousness* (the way we live) should catch up with our *declared righteousness* (our position in Christ). He starts chapter 4 by saying: *"I urge you to live a life worthy of the calling you have received."*

Did I come down from that mountaintop feeling intimidated and scared? No, I felt victorious! Victors think, talk, and behave in a certain way. Their language does not communicate despair, hopelessness, fear, or defeat. Paul is saying to us: "You are victors, seated with Christ at the top of the mountain. Behave like victors. You are at the top; live like those who belong on top."

We are ambassadors of the almighty God, each in our own spheres of influence. We do not expect ambassadors of great nations to drive old cars, wear tattered clothes, or behave in a demeaning manner. God wants us to act like ambassadors. Some are ambassadors of Christ among the secular. Others are His ambassadors among nominal Christians. Others of us are ambassadors of Christ among Muslims. God has placed each of us in a unique setting and context. Wherever that may be, we need to live like His ambassadors every day because we are representing our King with our attitudes, words, and behavior.

How, specifically, should an ambassador live? Paul gives this description:

"In your anger do not sin: Do not let the sun go down while you are still angry, and do not give the devil a foothold. He who has been stealing must steal no longer, but must work, doing something useful with his own hands, that he may have something to share with those in need. [Notice the 180 degrees of transformation. The thief stops stealing and starts working so that he can give to those who are more needy.] *Do not let any unwholesome talk come out of your mouths, but only what is helpful for building others up according to their needs, that it may benefit those who listen. And do not grieve the Holy Spirit of God, with whom you were sealed for the day of redemption. Get rid of all bitterness, rage and anger, brawling and slander, along with every form of malice. Be kind and compassionate to one another, forgiving each other, just as in Christ God forgave you. . . . Among you there must not be even a hint of sexual immorality, or of any kind of impurity, or of greed, because these are improper for God's holy people. Nor should there be obscenity, foolish talk or coarse joking, which are out of place, but rather thanksgiving"* (Ephesians 4:26–32, 5:3–4).

A poor man was traveling on a big ship to another continent. He could afford only to buy the cheapest ticket available. So he brought bread, cheese, and canned food to eat during the trip, while everyone else ate at the ship's fancy restaurants. On the last day, just before their arrival, he discovered that every ticket on the ship entitled people to eat at the restaurants. Every ticket covered not only the cost of the travel but the cost of the food as well.

As a believer in Christ, are you living like this traveler? Are you missing out on your privileges? Although you are seated with Christ at the top of the mountain, does your lifestyle communicate defeat, fear, and insecurity? Remember that you are a princess or a prince because you are a *child of the King.* If you keep your eyes focused on God and your position in Christ, the discrepancy between your actual righteousness and your declared righteousness will decrease. Are you living as a prince or princess or as a beggar? Does your lifestyle attract people to your King or repulse them?

Please spend a few moments thinking and praying about your attitudes, your thought life, your words, and your behavior. Are you living a victorious or a defeated lifestyle? Do you compare yourself to others and feel you don't measure up? Do you have a preoccupation with feeling sorry for yourself? Ask yourself if you have been conceited and self-righteous, preaching at your family and friends without demonstrating a lifestyle that honors God. Do you need to ask forgiveness of anyone? What actions of love can you take toward those around you?

Victors in Christ

In Ephesians 6:10–24, the apostle Paul tells the saints at the top of the mountain to take a stand and not retreat. Remember what the man told us after we defeated the other boys? He said, "You are at the top; stay at the top."

Paul begins this section with these words: *"Be strong in the Lord and in his mighty power. Put on the full armor of God so that you can take your stand against the devil's schemes"* (Ephesians 6:10–11).

The Devil cannot bring us down from the top of the mountain. Because Christ cannot be defeated by the Enemy, you and I, my friend, should not be defeated by him either. The Devil knows this, which is why he resorts to deception. He cannot come to us with the truth. Instead, he tries to convince us that because we do not *feel* like we are at the top of the mountain, we are *not* at the top anymore. Will you see through his deception?

Paul tells the saints, including you and me, to put on the whole armor of God so that we can stand against the Devil's deception. Paul must have gotten this idea from the armor the Roman soldiers wore. What does our spiritual armor include?

"Finally, be strong in the Lord and in his mighty power. Put on the full armor of God so that you can take your stand against the devil's schemes. . . . Therefore put on the full armor of God, so that when the day of evil comes, you may be able to stand your ground, and after you have done everything, to stand. [Do you notice how many times the word "stand" is repeated? You are at the top of the mountain; stay at the top. Stand firm. Do not retreat. When you feel like you do not belong at the top, do not put your trust in those feelings. Put your trust in what God thinks of you and tells you.] *Stand firm then, with the belt of truth buckled around your waist* [live with a clear conscience], *with the breastplate of righteousness in place* [You are dressed with the robe of Christ's righteousness. He earned the 100 percent passing grade, and He

gave that righteousness to you. Believe this truth and live it. This is how you wear the breastplate of righteousness.], *and with your feet fitted with the readiness that comes from the gospel of peace.* [It is not a gospel of arguing or winning arguments. It is a gospel of peace. People are not usually tripped up by Christ but by our self-righteousness. Are you ready, my friend, to humbly and lovingly acknowledge Christ and His grace on your life to those who are around you?] *In addition to all this, take up the shield of faith, with which you can extinguish all the flaming arrows of the evil one.* [The Devil, the old landlord, will shoot arrows of doubt at you, saying: "Does God really care for you? Does He have time for you?" You can extinguish these arrows of doubt by believing God's promise.] *Take the helmet of salvation and the sword of the Spirit, which is the word of God."* [Get into the Bible. Read it, study it, meditate on it, and memorize its verses or passages. The "sword of the Spirit," the Word of God, is both a defensive and offensive weapon. How equipped are you with the Word of God, and how effective are you at using it?] (Ephesians 6:10–17).

Spend some time evaluating your life in light of the full armor. What are your strengths? Thank God for them. Is there an area in which you need to be strengthened? What practical steps do you need to take?

I hope, my friend, you will know the joy of living victoriously, living "at the top of the mountain." Your position is assured. In Christ, you are a saint, an ambassador, and a victor. These things are true, no matter how you feel. I pray you will live them out!

Reflection and Discussion Questions

1. As a child of God, what are your privileges as explained in Ephesians 1? Look also at chapters 2 and 3. What additional privileges do you have?
2. As you read Ephesians 4, 5, and 6:1–9, what do you learn about the attitudes, motivations, and behavior of God's children, His ambassadors?
3. As you look at Ephesians 6:13–17, how can you put on the full armor of God on a daily basis?

CHAPTER 15

THE FAMILY OF GOD

IN THE PREVIOUS CHAPTER, WE LOOKED AT OUR POSITION IN CHRIST and how that allows us to live as saints, ambassadors, and victors. In this chapter, we'll go even further in understanding our new position as followers of Christ. We'll see the kind of intimate, personal relationship God wants to have with us, His children. But first, let's remember where we came from.

On the descending escalator, we struggled with our defilement, shame, and guilt, with no hope for the present or the future. Then Christ visited our planet and earned the 100 percent passing grade for all of us who accept it. Christ also took all of our sins—all that we have ever committed or ever will commit—to the cross with Him. He paid the price for these sins and, in the process, defeated the Devil and his greatest weapon, death. Through Christ, God declared us righteous and put us on the moving walkway, or the top of the mountain to use our illustration from the previous chapter.

Now that we're on the top, can we ever be forced down, crushed again by the Devil? No! We may feel discouraged or defeated, but those are just feelings. Our position is unshakable. Even when we fall down, the moving walkway keeps carrying us. God may discipline us, but He will never leave or forsake us. Think of it this way: If a child breaks an expensive dish in her home, her parents might discipline her, but they will not expel her from the house and say, "You are no longer our daughter." Neither does God do this when we fall down.

GOD AS DADDY

We learned earlier that the legalistic Jews at the time of Jesus did not even dare to pronounce the name of God. They feared that they might abuse His name and break one of the Ten Commandments. At the same time, Jesus was teaching His disciples about the nature and character of God and that He is our Father, our Dad. He even told them to address him as, "Our Father who is in heaven."

Years ago, I was a teacher at a boarding school in Lebanon, where I had a student named Ibrahim. He and the other students lived at the school because their parents were working in Africa. One day a fight broke out between fanatical groups in our city. The sound of bullets shooting was terrifying. The school closed right away, and we managed to send most of the boarding students to the homes of their relatives in the neighboring towns and villages. I was responsible for those few who remained, including Ibrahim. We avoided the windows and tried to stay in the safer rooms of the school.

On the third day, Ibrahim and I were kneeling together next to his bed to pray. Ibrahim had surrendered his life to Christ a few months earlier and was growing steadily in his relationship with God. We did not have a clue what would happen that day or the next. Would the fighters come occupy the school? Would we be able to escape? Would we be killed? As Ibrahim prayed, with tears in his eyes and with the sound of shooting all around us, he got deeper and deeper in his intimacy with his heavenly Father. His prayer went something like this: "Lord, we do not know what is going to happen. Will we stay alive? Most of my friends have gone. Where can I go, Lord? Where can I hide? I am coming to You, my Father. I know You will never leave me, and You will be my shelter and my protection. You are my Father, my *Baba* ('Daddy')."

As I knelt next to him and listened to him pray, I strongly sensed that Ibrahim had reached a new depth in his relationship with God. He experienced God as his "Daddy." The amazing thing to me was that the Holy Spirit revealed this deep truth to Ibrahim even before he read about this idea in the New Testament. The letter to the Galatians says:

"Because you are sons, God sent the Spirit of his Son into our hearts, the Spirit who calls out, 'Abba [Daddy], *Father.' So you are no longer a slave, but a son; and since you are a son, God has made you also an heir"* (Galatians 4:6–7).

Years ago, the famous Muslim novelist Tawfic Al Hakim started writing a weekly newspaper editorial in Egypt with the title, "A Conversation with God." Immediately after his first editorial, legalistic Muslims began criticizing the writer so severely that he had to change the title. It was no longer "A Conversation *with* God" but "A Conversation *to* God." The legalistic Muslims felt that God was so transcendent that a human could never have a conversation with Him.

But Jesus showed us that God the Father welcomes our conversation with Him. Jesus taught us to call God "Abba" or "Daddy."

In Islam, there are 99 attributes, or most beautiful names, for God. The Bible agrees with almost all of them. But the great news is that the Bible has another: God as our Father. He is the Father, and He wants to have a very big family of sons and daughters who are like Jesus. I know this might be difficult to believe, but it is the truth. Do not miss out on it, my friend. God longs to hear you call Him *"Baba"* or *"Daddy."*

Can you do this? When you pray, can you call God "Father" or "Daddy"? Try it out. It might be hard for you at first, but it will become more comfortable in time. It is also wise for you to know what to say and not say about this subject to your Muslim family and friends. It is a very hard concept for many people.

BROTHERS AND SISTERS IN CHRIST

If you have surrendered your life to Christ, your relationship is not only with God, your Father, but with brothers and sisters from a diversity of religious backgrounds, races, languages, and nationalities. This family is called the household of God *(ahl beit Allah).*

"You are no longer foreigners and aliens, but fellow citizens with God's people and members of God's household, built on the foundation of the apostles and prophets, with Christ Jesus himself as the chief cornerstone" (Ephesians 2:19–20).

In this new family there are no second-class citizens, no distinctions in race, religion, gender, or social status. We are all equal in God's sight. During the time of the early church, the status of Gentile believers was questioned by some of the Christians who came from zealous Jewish backgrounds. Paul confronted them to their faces in the city of Antioch. Later, in the Council of Jerusalem (Acts 15), the church elders decided that there was no distinction among God's people. The apostle Paul put it in these words:

"There is neither Jew nor Greek, slave nor free, male nor female, for you are all one in Christ Jesus" (Galatians 3:28).

This is the truth, although most of the time this is not lived out by those of us who carry Christ's name.

How deep is this relationship we have with fellow believers in God's family? We can answer this question by looking at a strange incident in Matthew 12:46–50.

"While Jesus was still talking to the crowd, his mother and brothers stood outside, wanting to speak to him. Someone told him, 'Your mother and brothers are standing outside, wanting to speak to you.' He replied to him, 'Who is my mother, and who are my brothers?' Pointing to his

disciples, he said, 'Here are my mother and my brothers. For whoever does the will of my Father in heaven is my brother and sister and mother.''

Can you imagine this situation? How do you think Peter, James, John, and the other disciples felt when Jesus treated them as top priority, calling them "my brother and sister and mother"? If Jesus pointed to you and called you His sister or brother, how would you feel?

To better understand how close this relationship is, let us imagine that I have two brothers. One is a committed follower of Christ, and the other is not. My relationship with the brother who is not a believer is based on the fact that we belong to the same family. We share the same parents and grew up in the same home. Over the years, this brother gets married and starts his own family, and I do the same. With time, our relationship as brothers evolves and changes. With our focus on work and our families, we do not have much time to see each other and deepen our relationship. The major tie that continues to bind us is our love and concern for our elderly parents, and our conversations are usually about family issues. Some day our parents will die, weakening our bond, and eventually we will die. Death will terminate our relationship forever. But this is not the case with the other brother, who is a follower of Christ.

With that brother, the situation is very different. Of course I will have with him all the family ties that I have with the other brother. But we both have become sons of God by surrendering our lives to Christ. Our fellowship takes a greater depth as we relate transparently to one another, not only on a social level, but also on other levels. We have the same heavenly Father, and our relationship as brothers in God's family will continue beyond death to eternity.

The incident in Matthew 12:46–50 teaches us that our relationships with our brothers and sisters in the family of God are more permanent and may even go even deeper than our relationships with our own earthly families.

If you have surrendered your life to Christ, you are a very valuable member of God's family. You are indispensable. Just as the eye, the ear, or the arm are crucial to the human body, so are you to the body of Christ. My friend, we need one another. I will be grateful if you pray for me. Pray that every day I will choose to listen to the new landlord and refuse to listen to the old one. I pray that you will be drawn closer to Christ as you are reading this book. I do hope that one day our paths will cross. If not on this earth, it will surely take place in heaven.

What a wonderful fellowship and relationship we can enjoy. We have the same goal and purpose, worshiping God and glorifying Him. We are praying for one another even though we have not met face-to-face. Most important, we share the same Father. We are in the same family, the family of God.

Welcome, my precious friend, to the family *(ahl bayt Allah)*—the household of God.

Reflection and Discussion Questions

1. Do you understand your position as a member of God's family? What does that mean to you?
2. We have often heard the expression that people are God's servants/slaves *('abeed Allah)*. Is it conceivable to you that we are God's children and that we can call Him *"Baba"*? Do you have difficulty calling Him "Father"? Why or why not?
3. What does it mean to you to belong to the household of God *(ahl bayt Allah)*?
4. What are some of the privileges and responsibilities of belonging to this great family?

CHAPTER 16

THE ABSOLUTE
ESSENTIALS

BEING BORN OF GOD, ALSO KNOWN AS BEING BORN AGAIN, IS THE beginning of new spiritual life. It is similar to the beginning of a new physical life. Before a baby is born, there is conception, then a period of gestation that usually lasts up to nine months, followed by birth. The actual birth may only last minutes, but growth takes a lifetime.

Spiritual birth includes a period of preparation for the encounter with Christ, during which time the person becomes unshackled from misconceptions and hindrances. At times the spiritual birth is easy, decisive, and memorable; at other times it is more a process of realizing the truth in stages. Like physical growth, spiritual growth also takes a lifetime.

If you have experienced the miracle of being born of God, what form did it take? Was it a decisive event, or was it more like a process of gradually realizing the truth? It does not make much difference. What really matters is being certain of your relationship with God, knowing that He is your Father, and being convinced that you belong in His family.

As we consider the absolute essentials for healthy spiritual growth, I will continue to use the illustration of a newborn baby. Let's think about what an infant needs to survive and grow:

- Breathing
- Water
- Healthy food
- Sleep
- Protection from germs and infections
- Quick treatment of disease
- Exercise and movement
- A parent or caregiver

To grow and mature in our relationship with God also require some absolute essentials. These spiritual essentials are to some extent parallel to the physical essentials a baby needs. Of course in some ways this comparison falls short. For example, we meet many of our body's physical needs spontaneously. We do not need to be convinced that breathing is essential for survival. We do it day in, day out, moment by moment, even during sleep, every second of our lives. Our spiritual needs are different. We must have an awareness of the need and make a conscious effort to meet it. This is one of the differences between physical and spiritual growth, and others will probably become apparent as we move ahead. Still, let's focus on the similarities in an effort to better understand the absolute essentials for spiritual growth to occur.

What are these essentials? What does a new follower of Christ need in order to grow?

- Prayer—our spiritual breathing
- A thirst for Christ
- The Word of God—our spiritual food
- Spiritual rest—trusting Jesus and casting our cares on Him
- Protection from doubts and the Devil's attacks
- Quick deliverance from sin and its effects
- Spiritual movement—acknowledging Christ and drawing people to Him
- A spiritual father or mother

In this chapter, we will examine the first two on this list.

Prayer: Spiritual Breathing

No human being can survive long without breathing, and a new follower of Christ can't survive without communicating with God through prayer. Prayer is not a duty *(fard)* that we perform once, twice, or even five times a day, and then live the rest of the day disconnected from God. Prayer is spiritual *breathing;* it is continuous communion with God. The apostle Paul put it this way:

"Pray in the Spirit on all occasions with all kinds of prayers and requests. With this in mind, be alert and always keep on praying for all the saints" (Ephesians 6:18).

Islam has two forms of prayer, *Salaat* and *Du'aa'*. *Salaat* is the ceremonial prayer done five times a day at set times and in set forms. *Du'aa'* is calling on God spontaneously and continuously and acknowledging our need for Him and our dependence on Him. Spiritual breathing is the *Du'aa'* form of prayer.

When we breathe, we inhale and exhale. With each inhalation, oxygen enters the body, contributing to many functions and chemical reactions. With each exhalation, the poisonous carbon dioxide comes out of the body.

Spiritual breathing involves inhalation and exhalation as well. Unlike physical exhalation, which is *continuous,* spiritual exhalation is *periodic.* We do it whenever we become aware of any sin in our lives. Please remember that we do not ask God for forgiveness in an attempt to gain His acceptance. He has already accepted us. We repent because we do not want anything to spoil our relationship with Him. We need to immediately get rid of poisons in our body that come as a result of unconfessed sins—big or small—related to thoughts, attitudes, or behavior. One of the verses that I memorized early on and practice all the time is 1 John 1:9. I referred to it in an earlier chapter.

"If we confess our sins, he is faithful and just and will forgive us our sins and purify us from all unrighteousness."

You might use this verse several times a day. Do not allow one unconfessed sin to stay in your life and spread its poison.

Spiritual inhalation means asking the Holy Spirit who dwells in us to control us and fill us. Jesus described this dependence on Him by referring to Himself as the vine, while we are the branches. Our survival as branches is dependent on our abiding in Him in an enduring, trusting relationship. Jesus said:

"'Remain in me, and I will remain in you. No branch can bear fruit by itself; it must remain in the vine. Neither can you bear fruit unless you remain in me. I am the vine; you are the branches. If a man remains in me and I in him, he will bear much fruit; apart from me you can do nothing'" (John 15:4–5).

The speed of our growth and maturity is directly proportionate to how much we continually depend on Him, trust Him, and ask the Holy Spirit to fill us and control us.

We inhale and exhale nonstop our entire lives. This is how it should be with spiritual breathing also—continually getting rid of everything poisonous and inhaling a dependence on God.

A THIRST FOR GOD

Water makes up about 60 percent of our bodies, and we cannot live long without it. Water cleanses, lubricates, and maintains our blood pressure and general health.

Christ referred to Himself as the "water of life" in Revelation 21:6, but it is His message in John 7 that provides us with a complete understanding of this metaphor. During one of the Jewish festivals, on the last feast day, a remarkable ceremony was performed. The priest brought in golden vessels filled with water from a stream that flowed under the temple-mountain and poured it on the altar. Then the people sang the words of Isaiah 12:3: *"With joy you will draw water from the wells of salvation."* The people were filled with ecstasy and joy during that ceremony.

On the last and greatest day of that feast, Jesus stood on a high place in the temple courtyard where everyone could see and hear Him. Then He said in a loud voice, *"If anyone is thirsty, let him come to me and drink. Whoever believes in me, as the Scripture has said, streams of living water will flow from within him"* (John 7:37–38).

Another time, Jesus made the same proclamation privately to a Samaritan woman. The woman came to draw water from a well, and Jesus asked her for a drink. After a long conversation with her, the offer was reversed. Instead of Jesus asking for a drink, He offered her the opportunity to drink of the Living Water.

"Everyone who drinks this water will be thirsty again, but whoever drinks the water I give him will never thirst. Indeed, the water I give him will become in him a spring of water welling up to eternal life" (John 4:13–14).

Do you have a thirst for Christ? Ask God to create within you a greater and stronger thirst for Him. One of the ways to express your thirst for God is to use the Psalms in the Old Testament. Many of these Psalms were written by David, who described his thirst for God with these words:

"O God, you are my God, earnestly I seek you; my soul thirsts for you, my body longs for you, in a dry and weary land where there is no water. . . . Because your love is better than life, my lips will glorify you. I will praise you as long as I live. . . . On my bed I remember you; I think of you through the watches of the night. Because you are my help, I sing in the shadow of your wings. My soul clings to you; your right hand upholds me" (Psalm 63:1, 3–4, 6–8).[1]

Sometimes I write down my own prayers in a special notebook. At times when I am struggling with a certain issue, I write down a "psalm" in that notebook describing to God my feelings, my agonies, and my

---

1 See also Psalms 62 and 27.

longings. At other times, when I feel like I am bursting with gratitude to God for His love and mercy, I write down another kind of psalm. In the space below, write your "psalm" to God. These might be prose or poetry. Tell Him exactly how you feel about Him. Share with Him your frustrations and ask Him for help. Describe to Him your inner longings and your deep thirst. Ask Christ to fill you with Himself, the Living Water.[2]

_____

_____

_____

_____

_____

_____

_____

_____

In the next chapter, we will continue to look at more of the spiritual essentials.

REFLECTION AND DISCUSSION QUESTIONS

1. Are the comparisons between the needs of a physical baby and a spiritual baby helpful? How?
2. How is your "spiritual breathing" going? Do you get rid of poisonous sins immediately, or do you tend to hold onto unconfessed sin for hours or even days?
3. How would you describe your dependence on God and your thirst for Him?

---

2 I would love to read some of the psalms that you write. Send them to me at this e-mail address: drjabbour@nabeeljabbour.com.

CHAPTER 17

SPIRITUAL FOOD

AND REST

IN THE PREVIOUS CHAPTER, I DREW PARALLELS BETWEEN THE NEEDS OF a newborn baby and a spiritual newborn, a new child of God. We focused on spiritual "breathing," or prayer. We also covered our need to thirst for God and how Christ is our Living Water. In this chapter, we will look at our need for proper spiritual nutrition and rest.

THE WORD OF GOD: OUR SPIRITUAL FOOD

The healthiest spiritual food we can ingest is the Word of God, the Bible. It is called the sword of the Spirit, the good seed planted in the field, a light to our feet, and a mirror that shows us our shortcomings. The psalmist compares the Word of God to delicious food: *"How sweet are your words to my taste, sweeter than honey to my mouth!"* (Psalm 119:103).

The prophet Jeremiah used this word picture as well: *"When your words came, I ate them; they were my joy and my heart's delight"* (Jeremiah 15:16).

There are many similarities between the good food we eat and the Word of God, our spiritual food, but there is also a huge difference. With physical food, the less we eat and the longer we fast, the hungrier we get. But with spiritual food, the Word of God, the *more* we eat, the more we hunger for it. If we starve ourselves from the Word of God, we will lose our appetite for it.

The apostle Peter exhorted the followers of Christ in the first century to crave the Word of God the same way babies crave milk.

"Like newborn babies, crave pure spiritual milk, so that by it you may grow up in your salvation, now that you have tasted that the Lord is good" (1 Peter 2:2–3).

According to this passage, you can do something about increasing your appetite for the Word of God. Peter used the verb "crave." The opposite of craving something is not having any taste for it. Being passive and not spending time in the Word of God does not increase your craving; it kills it. You can increase your craving by reading the Bible every day and by thinking and meditating over what you read. The more you "chew" on the words and the more you meditate on them and put them into practice, the more alive you feel and the hungrier you are to read more. Psalm 1 describes the person who delights in the Word of God as a tree planted by the riverside, bearing fresh fruit every month, never dropping a leaf, and always in bloom.

When God looks at His precious children, He sees some who are spiritually starving, sick, and malnourished. It must break His heart to see our dependence on others who must chew the Word of God for us and put it in our mouths because we are not willing to do it for ourselves. We must not allow ourselves only to be spoon-fed by others.

My prayer, my friend, is that your generation will be stronger than mine and that your love for God will be more fervent than mine. May your craving for God's Word be so strong that people around you catch your excitement and desire to get into the Bible to see Jesus.

In Part III of this book, you will find many helpful suggestions to take you deeper into the Word of God. It is a manual. It is not just for reading; it is for doing. If you buy a new watch, you will get a manual with it. That manual is not for mere reading. It is for discovering the capacities of your new watch and figuring out how to operate it. I do hope that you have already started using the manual and that you are building godly habits for the rest of your life.

Spiritual Rest

We find spiritual rest when we trust God and cast our concerns on Him. I used to think that trusting God was something I needed to learn as a young believer, and then I would "graduate" and move on to new areas of growth. But I am finding, more and more, that I never graduate from learning the kind of trust God wants me to have. At times, I need to focus on trusting God for certain relationships; at another time, I need to trust Him for our financial needs. At still another time, I need to trust God for my family and my work. And now, as I am getting older, I find that one of the biggest trust areas is for my health.

All humans are created with a few basic needs, and these are some of the hardest to trust God with. Among them are *the need to be loved* and *the need for significance*. When I struggle to meet these needs on my own, I am sapped of energy, and I lose my joy in Christ. On the other hand, when I find my satisfaction in God's love and in His hand guiding my life, I am filled with energy, serenity, security, and joy—rejuvenating rest in Christ.

Let's examine these two needs a bit closer and see how Christ meets them for us to give us His rest.

The Need to Be Loved

Author Philip Yancey described grace with these two sentences: *"There is nothing I can do to make God love me more. There is nothing I can do to make God love me less."*[1] I believe these two profound statements should be memorized and meditated on because they hold significant truth that can affect the way we think and live.

There is nothing you can do to make God love you more. You cannot earn more love from God. He loves you with a perfect love that cannot be increased any more. Remember what I have said about how God sees you. You are wrapped from head to toe with the robe of Christ's righteousness. When He looks at you, He sees Christ. Is Christ fully pleasing to God? Of course He is. And that is how He sees you too.

Of course the Devil will tell you that God would be happier with you if you read the Bible more and memorized more verses. But be assured this is the Devil's message to you, not God's. He *cannot* love you any more than He already does. Do not strive to *please* Him; strive to *trust* Him. The difference between these two words, *please* and *trust*, is huge. Get into the Word of God not with the motive of earning His love and trying to please Him. Practice these disciplines in response to His love by trusting Him that He is already pleased.

Disciplines such as reading and memorizing God's Word will contribute to your growth, but they are called disciplines of *grace*—not disciplines of *striving*. Please remember that grace does not mean that God relaxes His standards and accepts us as we are. Grace means that God showers His blessings through Christ to people who deserve His curse and wrath.

The second phrase is as profound as the first one and perhaps even harder to believe: *"There is nothing you can do to make God love you less."* When Jesus hung on that cross, He was accused of every sin you have ever committed or ever will commit. Your defilement *(najasa)* was poured on Him. He took upon Himself your shame and guilt. You do not need to

---

1 Philip Yancey, *What's So Amazing About Grace?* (Grand Rapids: Zondervan, 1997), 70.

hide from God like Adam did after he fell in sin. When you face the truth and come to God with something so awful that you find it hard to even admit to God, be assured of His response: "It is OK. It is all taken care of. Jesus was punished in your place for that. Be assured that I do not and will not condemn you. I was not even shocked by what you did. I knew what you did was wrong all along, but it is good that you know it too."

You can be sure of God's love for you.

The Need for Significance

Human beings long to make an impact and have a sense of purpose and adequacy. People all over the world, and especially in my Arab culture, fear losing dignity. We want to know we are valuable.

Some people do certain things to feel and to appear to others that they are significant. Others might do the same things because they are already secure and have a sense of significance. The great illustration that comes to my mind is the movie *Chariots of Fire*. It is the true story of two British runners who competed in the 1924 Summer Olympics in Paris. Eric Liddel was a devout Scottish missionary who ran because he knew it pleased God. Harold Abrahams was a Jewish student at Cambridge who ran for fame and to escape racial prejudice. Both men won their respective races, but what a difference between the two. One was overwhelmed with a sense of significance, and the other, sapped of energy, begged for significance.

What gives us significance? Here is a short list:

1. Knowing our intrinsic value. Remember that you are a prince or princess. Believe that and live it—not just an hour a week, but every day of your life. You are a child of the King of kings. You are an ambassador representing the almighty God. Believe that and live it.

I have a friend who comes from a Muslim background, who is imprisoned in a Third World country. He is in prison with many Muslim fundamentalists, as well as many politicians and leaders. He is not allowed to have his Bible with him, and his circumstances are very difficult. I am praying that he will remember he is the ambassador of Christ among his fellow prisoners and that he will live it. I am also praying 2 Corinthians 4:7 for him:

"We have this treasure in jars of clay to show that this all-surpassing power is from God and not from us."

He might feel very much like a cracked vessel of clay at this time, weak and disenchanted. But within him dwells the Spirit of God. The Holy Spirit can glow through his cracks as he lives his life among his fellow prisoners, honoring Christ. Like the apostle Paul, he can be an ambassador for Christ even in his cell. His life has value even there.

2. Giving meaning to the work we do. It is not what you do that gives you significance. Instead, you give significance to what you do because of who you are.

I heard the story of three men working next to one another carving stones for a building. When they were asked separately the same question: "What are you doing?" each gave a different answer. The first said, "I am doing this job because it is the only work that I know how to do, and I hate it." The second man said, "I am making money for my family." The third man's response was, "I am contributing to building a great palace with beautiful architecture. It might last for generations." How do you see yourself, my friend?

Do not underestimate how God uniquely designed you and gave you a job to do on this earth as His ambassador.

3. Having a goal for the future. When someone loses hope for the future, life becomes unbearable. Victor Frankel, a psychiatrist who spent years in the German concentration camps during World War II, made some significant observations about his fellow prisoners. A sick prisoner dying of typhus had a dream that the war would be over by Christmas. The hope that came from that dream kept him alive and strong. As Christmas approached, the conditions of the war did not improve, and this man's dreams for release were dashed. By Christmas, he died, and the Nazi doctor reported that he died of typhus. Victor Frankel came to a different conclusion. He knew that this man was sick with typhus for a long time. It was when he lost hope for the future that the disease killed him.

What are you living for? The apostle Paul writes about where we can find our hope:

"Therefore we do not lose heart. Though outwardly we are wasting away, yet inwardly we are being renewed day by day. For our light and momentary troubles are achieving for us an eternal glory that far outweighs them all. So we fix our eyes not on what is seen, but on what is unseen. For what is seen is temporary, but what is unseen is eternal" (2 Corinthians 4:16–18).

Jesus' Offer of Rest

How is your walk with Christ so far? Have you grown tired and weary? Christ went through a long struggle on your behalf to take you off the descending escalator and place you on the moving walkway. Listen to His offer in Matthew 11:28–30 (from *The Message*):

"Are you tired? Worn out? Burned out on religion? Come to me. Get away with me and you'll recover your life. I'll show you how to take a real rest. Walk with me and work with me—watch how I do it. Learn the unforced rhythms of grace. I won't lay anything heavy or ill-fitting on you. Keep company with me and you'll learn to live freely and lightly.'"

In the first months of my relationship with Christ, I used to have a certain practice that I really enjoyed. Whenever I felt the worries beginning to choke me, I laid down on my bed and said this prayer: "Father, as I am sure that this bed is strong enough to carry me, I believe right now that you are carrying me with your strong arms, close to your chest. I want to roll my worries and my concerns over to you. Thank you for keeping me close to your chest." As I prayed this prayer, I immediately felt that my muscles were beginning to relax, and gradually, I felt my anxieties disappear. Now that is rest!

My friend, do you need to roll your worries over on Christ, who loves you? Take Him up on His offer to learn the unforced rhythms of grace. Learn what these words mean. He wants you to live freely and lightly. How does that sound to you?

Reflection and Discussion Questions

1. How would you evaluate your intake of the Word of God, your spiritual food?
2. Do you believe there is nothing you can do to make God love you more? If you struggle with this, what makes it hard to believe?
3. Do you believe there is nothing you can do to make God love you less? What makes this hard to believe?
4. What contributes most to your sense of significance? How does your relationship with God affirm and contribute to your sense of significance?

CHAPTER 18

PROTECTION FROM SPIRITUAL INFECTION

DO YOU FIND YOURSELF OVERWHELMED AT TIMES BY THE NUMBER OF demands people put on you? As a new follower of Christ, you may be getting advice, warnings, and instructions on what to do and not do. Though you know intellectually that you live in an environment of grace, you may at times feel squeezed into a box of legalism. The checklist imposed upon you may threaten to shackle you once again. It may help you to think of these demanding people like a young mother trying to keep her baby clean and protected from dangerous infections. Though she loves the baby and truly wants what is best for it, she may become possessive and controlling in an effort to protect it.

There will be others who also love you who will try to keep you from following Jesus. May God give you wisdom to know how to deal with both types of people.

Remember that the Devil is the enemy. *People are not your enemy; the Devil is their enemy and yours.* He is the one who looks for areas of vulnerability and tries to attack you with spiritual infections. People are not enemies that you need to hate. At times, the Devil might use people, but they still deserve to be treated with love, compassion, and forgiveness. If this simple principle were followed by individuals, many conflicts would be resolved. If it were followed by nations, many wars could be avoided.

To resist the Devil, we need to know his strategies. How does he attack us? What infections does he use? He has four primary tricks that all begin with the letter "D": doubt, discouragement, division, and diversion.

DOUBT

In Chapter 13, we talked extensively about the kinds of doubts the Devil tries to infect us with. When you feel the doubts creeping in, protect yourself by affirming and asserting your trust in God's promises. Affirm your trust in the "new landlord," and shut the door in the face of the "old landlord," who comes to destroy you. Refuse to listen to him. Practice this principle on a daily basis.

DISCOURAGEMENTS

Discouragement can come from a number of sources. It could be that the Devil is trying to poison us, or we may be discouraged by difficult circumstances that God has allowed in our lives to purify us. Because God loves us, He desires to purify us like gold. Gold is purified through fire. When exposed to heat, gold melts down, and the cheap metals separate from the pure gold. What are the cheap metals in our lives? They might be areas of sin, or they might be unimportant goals or petty concerns.

Maybe you have heard someone say, "Getting cancer was the best thing that ever happened to me." This is the purification process at work, separating the unimportant from the eternally important. By separating these out, He can grow and mature us. This purification process can be very painful, but knowing its source and its cause makes it easier for us to cope and persevere.

The Devil does not seek to purify us but to destroy us. He is the author of discouragement, whispering lies to us about God, ourselves, and other people.

No matter what their source, trying circumstances and the accompanying discouragement are a certainty in life. How, then, should we respond during these difficult times?

An old Arab proverb says, "Do not carry the ladder the wrong way." To understand what that means, imagine this situation. A family lives in a very crowded neighborhood in Cairo, Egypt. The son is sent to borrow a wooden ladder from his neighbors. This should not be too difficult, because the ladder is three meters high and weighs only 5 kilograms. However, if the young man carries the ladder the wrong way—across his shoulders—the burden becomes much greater. Carrying it the wrong way will require people in the crowded street to push and pull at the ladder to avoid being hurt. Because of all the resistance, that 5-kilogram ladder will suddenly feel like it weighs 50 kilograms. But if he carries it the right way, the ladder doesn't feel nearly as heavy.

Can you see how this illustration applies to our difficult circumstances? When we have the right attitude about God and about our circumstances, we carry a load that weighs no more than 5 kilograms. God's intention is to purify us through our difficult circumstances, and He allows us only to experience what we can bear, namely the "5 kilograms." Your "5 kilograms" might be very different from mine, because God designs for us what will uniquely stretch and grow us. When we do not have the right attitude about God and our circumstances, the weight of our problem increases until we find ourselves carrying a 50-kilogram ladder.

I have known this principle since my youth, yet I still struggle at times with a problem that has become 50 kilograms because of my rotten attitude. How are you doing, my friend, with your difficult circumstances? Are you carrying the right weight—the weight God has designed you to bear—or are you struggling because of your wrong attitudes toward God and your circumstances?

The apostle James gives some practical suggestions in his New Testament letter: *"Consider it pure joy, my brothers, whenever you face trials of many kinds, because you know that the testing of your faith develops perseverance.* [If you remember that God loves you and that He wants to purify you through the "heat" you are experiencing, your load will be only "5 kilograms" and you will be able to cope. Part of the maturing process is to go through the fire.] *Perseverance must finish its work so that you may be mature and complete, not lacking anything"* (James 1:2–4).

The definition of maturity, according to this text, is being able to cope with all circumstances. God's intention is for us to grow and mature so that we can cope with whatever we face without becoming discouraged. An attitude of gratitude goes a long way in keeping our load to 5 kilograms.

". . . give thanks in all circumstances, for this is God's will for you in Christ Jesus" (1 Thessalonians 5:18).

The apostle Paul seems to be saying that if you want to live in the center of God's will on a daily basis, you need to embrace your circumstances, trusting that God is in full control. Keeping your eyes on Him rather than on your circumstances is the starting point for developing a grateful attitude.

As soon as you realize the Devil is the source of your discouragement, remember your position in Christ: You are seated with Christ at the top of the mountain, and you are carried by grace on the moving walkway.

DIVISION

As you look at Christianity, with its many denominations and churches, how do you feel? Sadly, you may see more division than you see cooperation and submission to one another. Division among Christians often occurs because of differences in doctrine or biblical interpretations. Other times, though, the divisions form when people become intolerant of one another because of personal issues and an attitude of rebelliousness.

Submission is one of the most important qualities taught in the Bible. It is the key to many human relationships, especially in marriage and family. We see it as well in the context of work and government. But what is submission, exactly, and how does it protect us from the divisions that threaten to infect our relationships?

There are two Arabic words that sound similar, yet their meanings are very different. *Khudou'* ("submission" in Arabic) is a beautiful quality, but it is often confused with passivity and slavishness, *Khunou'* in Arabic. *Khunou'* is more like a figure of speech you have probably heard: "being a doormat." It carries more a tone of subservience than godly submission.

Jesus was submissive to God the Father, as well as to the Roman governor and the religious leaders who wanted Him to die. His submission led Him voluntarily to the cross. But Jesus was not a doormat. He came to complete a mission, and He fulfilled it by going to the cross.

Many people assume that Christ was teaching subservience when He told His disciples to "turn the other cheek." What Jesus actually said was: *"Do not resist an evil person. If someone strikes you on the right cheek, turn to him the other also"* (Matthew 5:39). The following discussion of the cultural context of Jesus' time can help us understand what He was actually teaching:

> To hit someone on the right cheek assumes that the aggressor has hit the person with the back of his right hand. In the ancient customs of the land, this was considered a deep insult. This was how the powerful struck the powerless, the way a master struck his slave, or a Roman struck a Jew. But a blow administered with an open hand on the left side of the face was a blow struck at an equal. The difference between the two types of blows was actually codified in Jerusalem's local law at the time according to some historians. A backhanded slap to the right cheek of a man's peer was grounds to sue for punitive damages. The fine for a backhanded blow to a peer was 100 times the fine for a blow with the forehand. If a backhand was delivered to an underling, however, there was no fine. So when Jesus said to offer the left cheek, by this historical interpretation he wasn't prescribing a blind, masochistic pacifism. He was telling his followers, effectively, Confront the person offending you, forcing him to face you as

an equal, but do not respond with violence in return. That, in the context of Jesus' time and the social and legal codes that existed then, was a radical act of defiance. It turned the tables, forcing the stricken to accept the humanity and the equality of the one he was striking, even if he was not legally, or militarily, or politically, or economically recognized as an equal.[1]

Division is a serious infection, and submission is our best protection. The opposite of submission, rebellion, comes as a result of not trusting God's sovereignty over all circumstances. The rebel looks at the circumstances with anger, refusing to give in. People like this end up blaming everyone else for their difficulties and deceiving themselves about their own responsibility.

Subservient people, on the other hand, bow to everyone else in unhealthy ways and end up overwhelmed by their circumstances. Both the rebel and the doormat are not aware of God and what He is doing in their lives.

To live in submission is to be very much aware of God and what He is doing in our lives. Submission means surrender to God and trusting Him who is all powerful and all loving to take care of us, even in the midst of hard relationships. Do not let the Devil infect you with divisiveness. He does not want to see God's children living in humble submission to one another. He wants pride and division to get in the way. Protect yourself against this type of infection.

Diversion

When the Devil fails to trap you through doubt, discouragement, and division, he uses a fourth strategy, diversion. He diverts you from your important priorities and drives you to pursue secondary goals. Many of God's people have fallen into this trap. For example, some new believers become attracted to glamorous ministries and being in the spotlight too soon instead of developing in character and Christlikeness. A new believer, especially someone from a Muslim background, may become consumed with invitations to share his testimony in churches. But God may want him to stay focused on living with humility, putting others before himself, and serving his parents in the home.

We must be careful not to let the good take the place of the best. We assume that the enemy of the best is the bad. That is true, but a more

---

1 Colin Chapman, *Whose Holy City? Jerusalem and the Future of Peace in the Middle East* (Grand Rapids: Baker Books, 2005), 201.

dangerous enemy could be the good, because it looks harmless. We could spend hours doing good Christian activities while completely neglecting the best—connecting with God and developing an intimate relationship with Him.

What are your priorities, my friend? I would recommend the following for a new follower of Christ:

- Maintaining a close walk with God, trusting and obeying Him on a daily basis. This also includes shutting the door in the face of the old landlord and not listening to his lies.
- Cleaning the channels of your relationships with people. This includes demonstrating the transformation taking place in your life before beginning to articulate the Gospel with humility and love.
- Being a faithful steward of the responsibilities He has entrusted to you. If you are a student, be the best possible student, and study for Jesus as if He were your teacher. The same applies to work and family responsibilities.

May God help you stay right on track and not get distracted by the good in your pursuit of the best.

Reflection and Discussion Questions

1. How can you face difficult circumstances with a "5-kilogram" load? How do you keep it from becoming "50 kilograms"?
2. What Bible passages have you found that can help you cope with suffering?
3. What are the similarities between being a rebel and being subservient, like a doormat? How is submission different from both?
4. What are your top priorities? What threatens to distract you from these?

CHAPTER 19

TREATMENT OF
SPIRITUAL INFECTION

THOUGH IT IS IMPORTANT TO PROTECT OURSELVES AS MUCH AS POSSIBLE from the diseases the Devil tries to infect us with, infections are still a part of life on earth. Even though you are doing your best to listen to the new landlord and shut the door in the face of the old landlord, sin will still occur in your life. In this chapter, we will deal with how to treat "infections" when they break out.

Sin is all around us, and many temptations can lead us into sin. These may be as overt as committing a crime or as subtle as gossiping about a neighbor. Still, both are sin—infections that threaten our growing relationship with Christ. When God looks from His throne at His beloved children, what does He see? I do hope He sees that many of His children are healthy and growing. But what about those who are struggling with spiritual infections as a result of sin in their lives? The following illustration may help us imagine what God sees.

Years ago, hunters in the North Pole used innovative methods to hunt bears, such as using the ribs of animals as bait. The hunter would sharpen each rib on both ends, then bend the rib in a "U" shape. Then he would wrap meat around the bent rib, tie it with a strong string, and let it freeze in the snow. After untying the string, the hunter would bait the bears with this frozen meat. As soon as the bear smelled the meat, it would swallow the ribs one after the other without chewing the meat. Once the meat defrosted in the bear's stomach, the sharp ribs would snap out and pierce the bear's stomach. All the hunter had to do was wait until the bear collapsed with pain, and then he would finish it off.

Can you imagine how God must feel when He sees His beloved children swallowing the bait the Devil places around us? How sad it must be for the Father to watch our sin pierce our insides.

Even within the body of Christ, we have come to consider those who live with a clear conscience as unusual. Anyone who refuses to swallow "sharp ribs," or who gets rid of these "ribs" right away, is seen as someone rare. It has become normal to see His followers living daily under the burden of sin, shackled and in bondage. For many, having a clear conscience has become an occasional experience, a luxury, rather than a way of life. How tragic! We consider the sick and the weak the norm and the healthy as the exception.

When followers of Christ live without a clear conscience, shame and guilt sap them of their joy. They are like a car owner who has a hole in the gas tank of his car. The tank constantly leaks, and every few hours he has to refill the tank with gas. Sooner or later, he will get tired of this car and stop using it. Being a follower of God without having a clear conscience is a burdensome life.

Although there are many types of sin and every individual has his or her own unique temptations, I have observed that the most common infections occur in the areas of our relationships and how we deal with sexual temptations.

RELATIONAL SIN

Think for a minute about your relationships. Is there a relationship you need to restore? Are you willing to do the hard work to make this happen? It might require giving up your pride.

A few months after I surrendered my life to Christ, I was on summer vacation enjoying deep intimacy with Christ. Then I realized I had "swallowed a rib" a few months earlier during the school year. I had borrowed a nice necktie from one of my friends at school, and I intentionally "forgot" to give it back to him. As I thought about it that summer, I finally had the courage and honesty to call it by its true name. I admitted to God and to myself that I stole the tie. Although it was painful, I wrote a letter to my friend, put some money in the envelope, and sent it to him. Relief and joy came immediately. I felt like I was running, not just walking, on the moving walkway.

Jesus had a lot to say about relationships. Imagine a man traveling for a few days from north of Palestine to Jerusalem to worship and offer a sacrifice. After this very long trip, he may have arrived in Jerusalem just in time to hear Jesus say this:

"*Therefore, if you are offering your gift at the altar and there remember that your brother has something against you, leave your gift there in front of the altar. First go and be reconciled to your brother; then come and offer your gift*" (Matthew 5:23–24).

Jesus says to this man: If you want to really make your sacrifice count in God's eyes, leave the lamb—the sacrifice you brought with you from your home—here in Jerusalem. Travel back to your hometown, find the person you sinned against and ask for forgiveness, and then travel back to Jerusalem. After that you may offer your sacrifice. It would be like someone telling you to leave your Bible study group and go work on restoring a relationship before you join back in with the Bible study.

You might say, "But that person sinned against me; I did not sin against him. Is this my responsibility?" Addressing this situation, Jesus said: *"If your brother sins against you, go and show him his fault, just between the two of you. If he listens to you, you have won your brother over. But if he will not listen, take one or two others along. . . . If he refuses to listen to them, tell it to the church . . ."* (Matthew 18:15–17).

Either way, reconciliation is required. As you work to restore a relationship, keep in mind the following principles:

1. The goal is not simply to apologize; the goal is reconciliation. It is possible for you to apologize without resolving the conflict.

2. Before going to see the other person, spend time with God praying and remembering the details of the conflict. The sin of the other person will be very clear in your mind, but what about your sin?

"Why do you look at the speck of sawdust in your brother's eye and pay no attention to the plank in your own eye? How can you say to your brother, "Let me take the speck out of your eye," when all the time there is a plank in your own eye? You hypocrite, first take the plank out of your own eye, and then you will see clearly to remove the speck from your brother's eye" (Matthew 7:3–5).

Ask God to help you discover the "plank" in your own eye before you talk to the other person about his "speck of sawdust."

3. When you realize how you have sinned against the other person, determine to apologize to him. Do not mention his sin until he is willing to admit it.

4. When you apologize, do not say, "Sorry." Instead, say: "I have sinned against you in being selfish (or proud, or whatever the sin is). Will you please forgive me?" It is best to phrase your apology in the form of a question so that you get an answer. Ideally, the response will be, "Yes, I forgive you."

5. If the other person is willing to admit his sin, respond with humility and love.

Relationships are like a glass barrier that separates you from others. Your responsibility is to keep the glass clean from your side. You cannot force others to clean the glass from their side, but they may work on their side when they see you cleaning your side. When people see your humility, they are likely to respond in the same way.

Before you continue reading, spend time thinking and praying. If God brings to mind people with whom you need to reconcile, write down their names and start praying for the encounter. Ask God to prepare you both to experience Christ's presence during your talk.

SEXUAL SIN

A computer expert who loved the Lord told me he was asked to fix the computer of a Christian leader. As he worked on the computer, he discovered that the man had been viewing pornography on the Internet. When he finished fixing the computer, he told the man, "You have two problems on your computer. I fixed one, and you—with the help of God—need to fix the other." The computer stores images in its memory, and so do our brains. Exposing our minds to any type of pornography opens us up to dangerous spiritual infection. And, like the Christian leader, anyone can fall prey to this disease.

The Devil wants God's children to get hooked on pornography and other sexual sin so that he can control us with it. And how it must break the Father's heart to see His children struggling with this kind of sin.

How are you doing, my friend, in this area of your life? Are you struggling? If so, follow the three steps recommended in James 4:7: "*Submit yourselves, then, to God. Resist the devil, and he will flee from you.*"

1. Submit yourself to God. Surrender your total life to Him right now. Admit your guilt and shame. Plead to Him for help.

2. Resist the Devil. If you have pornographic magazines, burn them today. If you are tempted by pornography on the Internet, go to a follower of Christ you respect and tell him about your sin. Enter into an accountability relationship with him. Get an Internet program that filters any temptations. If you are involved in an ungodly sexual relationship—even if it is only in your mind—put an end to it. It is worth the money, the loss of face, and all that it takes to live with a clear conscience.

3. The Devil will flee from you. This is a promise! When you meet the first two conditions, the promise will follow.

In this chapter, we have looked at just two of the many types of sin that can infect us. Please remember that there is no money, nor pride, nor reputation worth preserving and protecting at the cost of living with a bad conscience. My friend, please stop reading and take care of the spiritual infections in your life. Start with your biggest battle, and the other ones will be easy. Once you conquer the Devil in one area, you will find that your trust in God will increase and you will experience victories in others.

REFLECTION AND DISCUSSION QUESTIONS

1. Did the illustration of hunting bears give you a new picture of sin and its effect on you?
2. Have you had the joy of experiencing a clear conscience since you surrendered to Christ? How would you describe that?
3. What spiritual infections do you need to deal with right now? How will you do it?
4. Do you have someone to hold you accountable to live as an ambassador of Christ? If not, who can you think of to fill this role?
5. Are you addicted to any particular sins? Accountability and discipline might be a temporary solution, but to go deeper you need to get to the root of the problem. Do you have someone who can help you do this?

Chapter 20

Exercise and Parental Care

One time when I was a child, I was confined to a hospital bed for several days. Although I had been physically fit prior to my hospital stay, afterward I could hardly get up to walk. It is amazing how fast atrophy sets in.

In this chapter, we'll look at the importance of exercising our spiritual muscles. We'll also consider the last of our spiritual essentials: the need for parental care.

Exercise and Movement

Exercise and movement are essential for good health and physical growth. Even after major surgery, patients today are encouraged to get up from bed as soon as possible and start walking. Movement keeps the body functioning properly.

Spiritual movement is equally important in the life of a new believer. We exercise our spiritual muscles by acknowledging Christ in a way that draws people to Him.

I made this discovery as a very new follower of Christ. I was in boarding school in Lebanon where half of my classmates were Muslim and half were Christian. A couple of days after my encounter with Christ, I was praying alone in my bedroom. I had a vague memory of a passage from the Bible that my mother read to me when I was a child. The passage was Matthew 5:23–24, which I mentioned in the previous chapter. In that passage, Jesus told a worshiper that before he offered his sacrifice in Jerusalem, he should first go back to his hometown to ask forgiveness from a person he had offended. Right then, I remembered a classmate whom I had not talked to for three years. His name was Ghassan, and I couldn't even remember the reason for our conflict.

Then a big struggle started in my head. I had thoroughly enjoyed my time so far with Jesus, and I wanted to maintain my relationship with Him at any cost. But when Ghassan came to mind, I lost my joy. How could I reconcile with him without any mediators? At our school, reconciliation occurred through a mutual friend who would volunteer to persuade one person to forgive the other. Then he would do the same with his other friend. Finally, with his help and the help of others, the two would meet in a neutral place to shake hands and break the ice without either one losing face. Well, it did not happen this way with Ghassan and me.

On that day, I struggled with my pride for a few minutes. Finally, I knelt next to my bed and promised my Lord that I would do anything to obey Him if He would help me. I vividly remember going down to the courtyard of the school with my heart racing. Ghassan was standing with two of his friends next to a tree. When I approached him, his face turned pale. I said, "Ghassan, I do not remember why we had a conflict three years ago. I want to apologize to you for the way I have offended you. Will you please forgive me?" And I reached out to shake his hand.

Without saying a word and with his face still very pale, he reached out and shook my hand. Then I told him that last Sunday I surrendered my life to Christ and out of obedience to Christ, I needed to be reconciled with him. Then I shook his hand again and ran up the stairs to my bedroom. I knelt next to my bed and, bursting with joy, thanked Christ for giving me the courage to obey Him.

Within hours, the news spread among my classmates. One came to me and wanted to know why I did what I did and whether I was a Christian or a Muslim. I told him that I was a Christian by name all my life, but since last Sunday I had become a follower of Christ by choice. From the first week of my new life in Christ, I started exercising my spiritual muscles. It has not always been easy to do this over the years, but what an adventure it has been!

John chapter 9 tells a beautiful story about a young man who was born blind but was healed by Jesus. After he was healed, people wanted to know what happened, so they came to this young man and asked him. He said to them: *"The man they call Jesus made some mud and put it on my eyes. He told me to go . . . and wash. So I went and washed, and then I could see"* (John 9:11).

He told a simple story of what Jesus did for him and how he was healed. The Pharisees focused on the fact that Jesus healed him on a Sabbath, rather than rejoicing with him for his healing. They interrogated the young man about what happened. He simply told them that he was blind and now he could see. The more he acknowledged Christ, the more courageous he became, until the Pharisees left him and went to intimidate his parents. The parents responded fearfully: *"'We know he is our son . . . and we know he was born blind. But how he can see now, or who opened his eyes, we don't know. Ask him. He is of age; he will speak for himself'"* (John 9:20–21). Unlike their son, they were afraid to acknowledge what Jesus had done. Instead, they chose the safe, easy way out to escape harassment from the Pharisees.

The book of Acts records the history of the early church's amazing growth. The energized followers of Christ did not ask God for opportunities to tell people about Christ. Instead, they prayed for boldness and courage. With courage, they discovered an abundance of opportunities to acknowledge Christ. And the more they acknowledged Him, the faster they grew.

One year, some friends of mine in the Middle East decided to study the topic of fear in the Bible. That study did wonders in their lives. When fear is broken, God can do anything through the lives of His children.

The Right Way to Exercise

Before you start exercising your spiritual muscles, be aware that there are wrong ways to acknowledge Christ.

One wrong way is to start speaking out right away with self-righteousness and pride, attacking the religion of those you are speaking with. Without a transformed life as evidence of what Christ has done in you, preaching at people turns them into enemies. Early on, I did this with some people, and I regret it to this day.

Another wrong way is for you to decide to become a silent, secret believer, motivated by fear rather than by courage, wisdom, and love. The Devil can choke you through your fears.

The right way to acknowledge Christ is to exercise courage and boldness, yet with humility and love. Ask God to transform your life on a daily basis. Clean the channels in your relationships so that the love of Jesus flows through them. What does that mean? Think of your family. Do they see you as a humble, loving person, who has a servant heart? Do they think of you as the peacemaker in the family? Or do they see you as a self-righteous religious freak who abandoned the family religion and traditions by converting to another religion? Do they see in your life *Christ* or the *wrappings*?

How have you been doing, my friend? Jesus considers you His ambassador. Have you been embarrassed to acknowledge your allegiance to your King? Or have you been too contentious and argumentative in your attempts to draw others to Jesus?

Spend a few minutes thinking about these questions and asking God what corrections need to be made.

PARENTAL CARE

When a family friend comes over to visit, he may enjoy playing with the young toddler in the home. But once the guest smells that the child needs a clean diaper, he sends him back to his parents. It is as if the friend is saying, "I love you as long as you are clean, but once you get messy, I am done with you."

Have you ever had this feeling? Are there people in your life who love you as long as you live in victory and your life in Christ is attractive? Do you feel like they push you away when you mess up and embarrass them?

To the followers of Christ in Corinth, the apostle Paul wrote:

"Even though you have ten thousand guardians in Christ, you do not have many fathers, for in Christ Jesus I became your father through the gospel" (1 Corinthians 4:15).

We might have many "teachers and guardians" who contribute to our spiritual lives, but fathers and mothers are much more rare. Parental care requires a great deal of love and involves a very special relationship. Paul described his relationship with the Thessalonians this way:

"We were gentle among you, like a mother caring for her little children. We loved you so much that we were delighted to share with you not only the gospel of God but our lives as well, because you had become so dear to us. . . . For you know that we dealt with each of you as a father deals with his own children, encouraging, comforting and urging you to live lives worthy of God, who calls you into his kingdom and glory" (1 Thessalonians 2:7–8, 11–12).

Think about the relationships you have made on your journey with Christ. Who have been your teachers and guardians? Have you ever expressed your gratitude to them for the way they helped you? Have you had the benefit of spiritual fathers or mothers who stuck with you even when you messed up? Have you had the blessing of having others pour out their lives for you at critical times in your journey with Christ? Have you been teachable to them, or have you resisted?

In the book of Acts, we read about Paul's journey with Christ and his lonely times. Because Paul was once a militant Jew and persecutor of Christians, when he came to Jerusalem, the followers of Christ there were afraid of him. But among them was a man with a father's heart named Barnabas who listened to Paul's story in great detail and believed in him. Barnabas went to the leaders of the church in Jerusalem and convinced them that Paul had become a new man and an authentic servant of Christ. Because Barnabas believed in Paul, the church leaders in Jerusalem started believing in him too. Then Paul went to his hometown of Tarsus, where he was alone for some time. There, God Himself cared for him and nurtured him. Barnabas later came back into his life, recruiting him to come to Antioch and help with the ministry there. On their first mission trip together, Barnabas allowed Paul to become the leader of the team. Barnabas, who had been the leader, was willing to become the follower of someone younger in the faith and in experience.

Paul later became a spiritual parent to many young followers of Christ, including a young man named Timothy. When you read Paul's letters to Timothy in the New Testament, you sense the kind of heart Paul had for him.

My friend, if you do not have a mentor, ask God to provide you with one, the right one. (It is better to have no mentor at all than have the wrong one.) This mentor could be the one who helped you encounter Christ. Or it might be someone else who shares your vision, someone willing to "adopt" you and stand with you through thick and thin. Be teachable to this mentor, and be transparent with him or her. If there is no one like this locally, find someone you admire who could mentor you long-distance through e-mail, phone calls, and periodic visits.

Now, consider the reverse picture. Has God given you a special relationship, but you did not carry the responsibility of caring for that person like you should have? It is never too late. Find someone to whom you can pass on all that you are learning, but be prepared to stick by them, messes and all. This is what a spiritual parent does.

Reflection and Discussion Questions

1. What is the relationship between boldness and opportunities in reaching out to those around you?
2. What are some wrong ways of doing evangelism? Have you done any of these? What were the consequences?
3. What right ways have you discovered to share your faith?
4. Do you have a mentor? If not, how will you find one? What qualities will you look for in that person?
5. Is there someone in your life you can mentor? How would you begin?

CHAPTER 21

THREE COMMITMENTS

IN THE LIFE OF EVERY NATION, CRITICAL DECISIONS ARE MADE, GOOD and bad, and people live with the consequences for generations to come. The same is true of individuals. The Bible is filled with examples of this. Ruth chose to stick by her mother-in-law Naomi, which led her to play a key role in Jesus' family lineage. Young David stepped out in faith to battle the giant Goliath when everyone else ran in fear. This was one big step on the path that led David to eventually be king.

But the greatest decision of all time, with the most far-reaching consequences, was Jesus' choice to go all the way to the cross. He could have ended His torture and suffering at any time, but instead He chose to persevere to the very end in order to accomplish His great mission. If Jesus had not persevered, how would the history of the world be different today, including your history and mine?

At critical times in our lives, we all come to a crossroads at which choices have to be made. As you walk on the straight road with Jesus, you will need to make some very important decisions regarding your commitment to Him. These decisions will affect the rest of your life. They will also affect the people you are influencing, including your family. Your decisions are these:

1. Will you commit yourself as a disciple of Christ to the last day of your life?
2. Will you commit yourself to the Bible as your standard of truth and your source for growth?
3. Will you commit yourself to be a loyal member in the family of God?

FREE WILL VS. GOD'S SOVEREIGNTY

God created the cosmos with such precision that the earth revolves around the sun, and our solar system revolves around the center of our galaxy. Can you imagine if our planet one day got tired of revolving around the sun and decided to "live for itself" instead, declaring its independence? What would happen? The result would be catastrophic, to say the least. Of course this will not happen because our planet is restrained. It operates under the sovereignty of God with no freedom to maneuver.

We, however, are different from the planets. We live under the "ceiling" of God's sovereignty, yet we walk on the "floor" of free choice. We are free to make our decisions, and we live with the consequences. Though it is a hard concept to grasp, God's sovereignty and our free choices are identical. This is the mystery called predestination. For example, He chose me before the foundation of the world, yet I chose to surrender my will to Christ and put my trust in Him. This great mystery only makes sense when we understand God's power and greatness.

COMMITMENT TO CHRIST

According to the Old Testament law *(shari'a),* a Hebrew master should set his Hebrew slave free after six years. He was not only to release him but to give generously to him so that he could make a good start on his own.

I would assume that every slave, when the opportunity came, wanted his freedom. Yet in the *shari'a,* we see the slave at a crossroads, facing two choices. One choice was to take his freedom and leave; the other is recorded in Deuteronomy 15:16–17:

"But if your servant says to you, 'I do not want to leave you,' because he loves you and your family and is well off with you, then take an awl and push it through his ear lobe into the door, and he will become your servant for life."

Each of us, in our journey with Christ, faces a similar decision. We have the freedom to walk away from our loving Master and go back to living on our own. Or we can choose to stay under His care, growing in Him and living the life He created us to live.

The illustration is one of slavery, but in reality, committing ourselves to this Master is choosing a life of true freedom. Christ does not call us slaves but friends. Are you willing to go to Jesus and ask Him to "pierce the lobe of your ear"? Are you willing to dedicate, or rededicate, your whole life to Christ? This commitment involves your relationships, your time, your priorities, your family, and all that you own. It could involve suffering, persecution, imprisonment, and even martyrdom.

Jesus told this parable, recorded in Matthew 13:45–46:

"'The kingdom of heaven is like a merchant looking for fine pearls. When he found one of great value, he went away and sold everything he had and bought it.'"

In this parable, Jesus is the pearl of great value. Let us say that I decide to come to God the Father and ask Him, "What is the cost of that Pearl?"

God answers: "All you have. How much is that?"

I would respond, "Well, I have some money in the bank, and I have some stocks and bonds."

"What else?" God asks. Then I would list all my assets, including my car.

"What else?" He asks again. I can only say, "All that is left is myself, my wife, and my children."

Then He says, "Go and put everything you own into a contract." I give Him everything, every last bit of myself, and then I begin to walk away.

But God calls out to me and says, "Here is your family. Take good care of them, because your wife is My daughter, and your children are My children. Furthermore, I am entrusting you with My car, My money, My stocks and bonds, and everything else you put in the contract. You are no longer the *owner*, but you are the *steward* of what belongs to Me."

The cost to follow Jesus is enormous. It requires everything in your life—every asset and every relationship. Are you willing to surrender them all to Jesus? Will you write a prayer to Jesus, telling Him why you want to become His "slave," by choice, forever?

COMMITMENT TO THE WORD OF GOD

The Bible contains 66 books—39 in the Old Testament and 27 in the New Testament. Approximately 40 writers participated in building this library over a period of 1,500 years. Yet, amazingly, the 66 books are tied together in unity, flow, and continuity. The central figure throughout the Bible is Jesus Christ. The Old Testament looks forward to His coming; the New Testament is a record of His visit and the story of His followers in the first century.

Paul wrote: *"All Scripture is God-breathed and is useful for teaching, rebuking, correcting and training in righteousness"* (2 Timothy 3:16).

All 66 books of the Bible are God-breathed. They are all *authored* by the Holy Spirit, who used different men over different periods of time to put the words on paper. This passage also gives four reasons why the Bible is crucial to our lives. It is used for:

- *Teaching.* It is the standard of truth *(Furkan).* It is the measuring stick, providing a standard for what is right and what is wrong. It provides instruction on what to believe, what to do, and what not to do.
- *Rebuking.* When we go in the wrong direction, the Word of God shows us what we have done wrong and brings us back in the right direction.

- *Correcting.* The Word shows us when and how to repent of our sin and how to return to close communion with God and with others.
- *Training in righteousness.* The Bible helps us do the right thing again and again until it becomes ingrained in our lives.

You might find it difficult to commit yourself to the Bible as the standard of truth *(Furkan)*, because there are things in it that you do not understand. Some things you will come to understand over time, but others you may only fully understand when you are in the presence of God. It is dangerous, however, to live with indecisiveness without establishing the Bible as your anchor of truth. Without it, you will be blown by the wind in every direction.

When I was in college, I went through a few difficult weeks because of a certain sin that I was not willing to confess and abandon. I rationalized that it was fine to be both a follower of Christ and at the same time continue to live with this sin. The philosophy classes I was taking at the time made the situation even more confusing. I wondered if I could even trust the Bible.

When I came to the end of myself and confessed my sin to God, I made the decision to commit myself by faith to the Word of God as my standard of truth. It was like a very tired person who had been standing up for weeks finally found a chair to sit on. Could I trust that chair? Would it break into pieces if I sat on it? By faith, I made the decision to "sit." I committed myself to the Word of God. What a difference that decision made in my life. The passage that helped me make that decision was Psalm 138:2. The American Standard Version (asv) of the Bible puts it bluntly:

"I will worship toward thy holy temple, And give thanks unto thy name for thy loving kindness and for thy truth: For thou hast magnified thy word above all thy name."

I was satisfied with what God said about His Word. He is as sure of it as He is of His own name and reputation. That was good enough for me.

Have you made a similar commitment to the Word of God as your standard of truth? This is a key decision to keep you walking in the right direction, toward the Father, on the moving walkway. However, I do not want you to think that just knowing biblical truth is the answer to all of the pain in your life. Experiencing biblical truth—and using it to replace the lies you have believed in the past—is the only way to deal with your pain.

For years, I occasionally felt that important people in my life did not love me, leaving me feeling abandoned and rejected. I tried to deal with these feelings with biblical truth, but the feelings continued. Then a friend helped me by praying, "Please, Lord, bring to Nabeel's mind the earliest and most traumatic experience in which he felt abandoned." After a time of silence, I remembered an incident from when I was two or three years old.

I went with my father and some other adults to visit friends, and for some reason, instead of taking me inside with them, they left me alone in the car. I was there for perhaps an hour, crying and sweating, assuming that I had been abandoned forever. My little mind could not comprehend that my father would soon be back for me. When he finally returned to the car, I was soaking with sweat and exhausted from crying. I vividly remember how guilty my father looked.

When I shared this story with my friend, I found myself crying again like that little boy. My friend told me to stay in the "room" of that painful experience and wait for God. I was tempted to get out of that "room" and go to the "room" of all the Bible verses I know. But by dealing with the painful memories, I was able to see the lies. I was not abandoned forever. I was not worthless and unworthy of love. I realized it was not the traumatic experience that was the problem, but the lies that I believed about the experience. When I visualized God there with me in the car, putting His arm around my shoulder and wiping away my tears, assuring me that He loved me and would never abandon me, the lies were demolished.

Renewing our minds with truth from the Bible is an important part of our emotional healing, but sometimes we must go to a deeper level for God to bring true healing. I pray you will find someone to help you go through this process if you have deep wounds from the past.

COMMITMENT TO THE FAMILY OF GOD

In an earlier chapter, I described the term "body of Christ" and how each of us, as a follower of Christ, plays a role in that. The New Testament uses another word picture to describe life in God's family. The picture is that of stones used to build a great edifice, the temple of the Holy Spirit.

"You also, like living stones, are being built into a spiritual house to be a holy priesthood, offering spiritual sacrifices acceptable to God through Jesus Christ" (1 Peter 2:5).

When we lived in Egypt, I learned to become a tour guide for the friends who visited us. I never stopped being amazed at the huge slabs of rock that were cut to just the perfect shape and used to build the temple of the Sphinx. So much work must have been done to the rocks before they were brought to the building site. The edges had to be straightened and the sides made smooth before the rocks could be used in the temple. Once each stone was ready, it was brought to the building site and placed in just the right place.

God is doing a work similar to this, using His people, you and me, as His living stones. Unlike the rocks used to build a physical structure, however, we are not a finished product before we are brought to the building site. Our rough edges are actually dealt with *after* we are placed in the wall with the other stones. The living stones in the temple of the Holy Spirit sharpen each other as they rub together.

Being placed in the wall while we are still an unfinished product helps in the smoothening process. God is working on us, shaping us to be more like Jesus. Sometimes He does this by using encouraging words from other people. Other times, He works on us through difficult circumstances. He may even use someone who always rubs us the wrong way. Proverbs 27:17 says, *"As iron sharpens iron, so one man sharpens another."*

You do not sharpen a knife by rubbing it on a banana peel. Difficult people and difficult circumstances in our lives are God's tools to make us like Christ.

I remember the last meeting I had with a man who had discipled me for years. He told me he believed that God wanted him to focus with me on three areas of weaknesses in my life. It was a difficult session, and I got very discouraged and overwhelmed with my weaknesses. Very soon afterward, a mutual friend came and sat with me. He knew what had happened. He opened his Bible to John 15 and read to me the following verses:

"'I am the true vine, and my Father is the gardener. He cuts off every branch in me that bears no fruit, while every branch that does bear fruit he prunes so that it will be even more fruitful. . . . I am the vine; you are the branches. If a man remains in me and I in him, he will bear much fruit; apart from me you can do nothing'" (John 15:1–2, 5).

What stood out to me as he read that passage was the phrase *"every branch that does bear fruit he prunes so that it will be even more fruitful."* I learned that because I was fruitful, God was pruning me so that I would become even more fruitful. Sometimes God uses other believers to prune us.

Do you allow people to be honest with you, my friend? Or do you keep people at arm's length, communicating to them that they should be very careful about what to say and what not to say to you? Do not miss out on the opportunities that God might be designing for your life. If you do not belong to a small group, look for a group of like-minded followers of Christ who share your background.

Another desire God has for us "living stones" is that we accept our place in the great building He is assembling. By becoming a small part of a big wall, we may fear losing the beauty of our individuality. Or some of us may feel like we deserve a more prominent place in the building. But living stones are not used for exhibition; they are used for building the temple of the Holy Spirit. The Holy Spirit decides what gifting we should have and where we fit in the edifice. Christ has the master plan, and He knows where each one of us fits. Some followers of Christ have an obvious function, and others have a more subtle function. Both are equally important.

We have looked in this chapter at three core commitments: (1) to be a disciple of Jesus to the last day of your life; (2) to look to the Bible as your standard of truth; and (3) to be a loyal member in the family of God. In order to stay on the moving walkway and enjoy the kind of life God wants for you, you must decide that you will make these commitments. Doing this will keep you walking on the straight road. These will likely be the most important decisions of your life.

REFLECTION AND DISCUSSION QUESTIONS

1. Have you had "the lobe of your ear pierced" for Christ? In other words, have you made the decision to commit your whole self—all that you have—to Jesus? If not, what is keeping you from doing this?

2. Have you committed yourself to the Bible as your source of truth? What helped you make that decision, or what is keeping you from making it?

3. Do you have a "sharpening" relationship with people in your life? Are there any difficult relationships God is using to deal with your rough edges?

4. Do you make it easy for others to share honestly with you?

5. Have you found your place as a living stone in the temple of the Holy Spirit? What do you think your gifts are in the body of Christ?

CHAPTER 22

THE BIG PICTURE

THANK YOU, MY FRIEND, FOR JOURNEYING WITH ME THROUGH THE previous two parts of this book. I hope that Part I played a role in unshackling you and showing you the truth about Jesus. Part II was aimed at helping you understand your new position in Christ and teaching you disciplines of grace to help you grow. The remainder of the book, Part III, is a manual intended to equip you with godly habits for a lifetime.

But first, I want to look with you at one more passage of Scripture that will give a final overview of all you have read in this book. This passage reveals the different stages of our journey with Christ, illuminating where you have been and where you are headed.

In his first letter, the apostle John wrote to three categories of people: children, young men, and fathers.

"I write to you, dear children, because your sins have been forgiven on account of his name. I write to you, fathers, because you have known him who is from the beginning. I write to you, young men, because you have overcome the evil one. I write to you, dear children, because you have known the Father. I write to you, fathers, because you have known him who is from the beginning. I write to you, young men, because you are strong, and the word of God lives in you, and you have overcome the evil one" (1 John 2:12–14).

CHILDREN

If we were to show a family photo to a little girl and ask her to tell us about it, what would she say? Probably she would start by pointing to herself, as she perceives herself to be the center of her family. Then she would point to her mother, father, sister, and brother. At this stage in life, everything revolves around her. If we show her this same family photo 30 years later, her response will likely be different.

In the family of God, young followers of Christ are very much like this little child. They see themselves as the center of their universe.

Everything revolves around them. Even God, they believe, is there to bless them, answer their prayers, heal them, and celebrate them. It is true that God does these things. He is not deceived about their nature and He knows they are unworthy, yet He celebrates that they are now cloaked in Christ's robe of righteousness.

About the children, John wrote: *Their sins have been forgiven, and they have known the Father.* Young followers of Christ need to be saturated with the truth of how special they are to God and how they have been completely forgiven. The more they are genuinely loved, appreciated, and accepted, the more they will grow to become healthy, mature people. Part I of this book focused on this stage, grounding the young follower of Christ in God's love.

For new believers, life is a celebration. They rejoice that all their sins have been forgiven. They celebrate that they get to live in the lap of their heavenly Father. I do hope, my friend, that throughout this book, and especially in Part I, you experienced this celebration.

Young Men and Women

It is normal for the little girl to see herself as the center of her universe and to act like a child. But as she grows to become a teenager, we expect her to leave behind her childish self-centeredness and move on to another stage of growth and maturity.

When children grow up knowing they are greatly loved and accepted, they usually grow up to become mature adults. The more a child's needs to be loved and treated with significance and dignity are met, the healthier this person's self-image will be as an adult.

The same applies to God's family. Once the new believer's needs are met in a deep way, this person is ready to graduate to another stage of maturity. The second stage, according to 1 John 2:12–14, is young manhood or young womanhood. This stage is described this way: *They have overcome the evil one, they are strong, and the word of God lives in them.* These qualities describe a disciple of Christ.

It is normal for toddlers to bump into tables and chairs and to fall down as they learn to walk. But as they grow, they learn how to avoid bumping into things. The same is true for followers of Christ as they become disciples. Not only do they learn to confess their sins, but they learn to avoid falling into sin in the first place. They begin to develop hatred for sin because of their growing love for God.

Young followers of Christ should come to the realization that they are not the center of the universe. Christ is the center, and His followers revolve around Him. With that important understanding, they can move toward commitment and discipleship. Parts II and III of this book are designed to help a new believer grow as a disciple.

Our text describes three qualities of a disciple. First, he has "overcome the evil one." A disciple has a good grasp of what Christ accomplished through His victory on the cross. A disciple knows the Devil was crushed and, in light of that fact, lives victoriously. He does not gaze at the Devil. He gazes at God, and glances at the Devil.

Another quality of a disciple is that the Word of God lives in him. A disciple is not like an infant, who must be fed by its mother. Finally, a disciple knows how to get into the Word of God on a daily basis. He not only reads it but also studies it, memorizes it, and meditates on it. A disciple of Christ is strong and healthy. He is walking steadily forward on the moving walkway.

FATHERS

When we come to the fathers in this passage from 1 John, we see only one phrase repeated twice. The fathers are those who have *"known him who is from the beginning."*

Fathers are those who have known Him, the heavenly Father, and have developed hearts like His. The Father loved His children even after they rebelled. He treated them with love even though they were unworthy. Do you remember the story Jesus told about the father with two sons (Luke 15:11–32)? He showed love to both sons, even though both were unworthy.

Earlier, I referred to one of my Muslim heroes, Rabi'a Al Adawiya. I quoted her famous prayer in Chapter 4, and I will paraphrase it again here: *"Lord, why do I love you? What is my motive for loving you? Do I love you because of a desire to go to paradise? If this is my motive, then deprive me of paradise. Or do I love you out of fear of going to hell? If this is my motive, then send me to hell. O Lord, please purify my motives. Help me to love you for your own sake because you are worthy of all my love and all my worship."*

Her prayer provides a platform to examine four levels of love. The first is the lowest, and the last is the highest.

- *Possessive love* is a self-centered kind of love that is possessive in nature. Lust is a form of this type of love.
- *Gratitude love* is higher than possessive love, but it has an element of selfishness to it. We love the people who love us. We give gifts to people who give us gifts. We love God because He first loved us.

- *Love of excellence* is still a higher level that is motivated by deep respect and recognition of qualities of excellence. In a huge university, a professor might lecture to hundreds of students. One of those students may love this professor so much that he reads every book the professor has written, yet the professor doesn't even know the student's name. I believe that Rabi'a Al Adawiya reached this stage in her love for God. She loved Him for His qualities of excellence. She puts me to shame in my shallow love for God.
- *Irrational love* is the highest form of love. It is beyond reason and cannot be explained. It can only be illustrated.

During our years in Egypt, I became friends with an engineer who was good with plumbing, electricity, and carpentry. Any time we had a problem in our apartment, he would come on his day off to fix it and make some extra money. Early in our relationship, he told me he had a severely mentally challenged daughter. I could tell how much he loved her by the way he talked about her.

One day he was fixing something in our apartment, and it turned out to be a big project. He needed to get a spare part from downtown Cairo, so I went with him to get it. On the way back, he needed to stop by his apartment to get a certain tool. As we were going up the stairs to his home, he started telling me how much he loved his daughter. She could not walk, talk, or eat by herself, although she was about seven years old. I wondered how I should relate to her if I saw her.

I did see her, and I vividly remember the encounter. When my friend opened the door, the girl was standing on the sofa, leaning against a wall. When she heard the voice of her father, she turned to look at him and broke into a big smile. Her eyes were crossed, and saliva leaked from her mouth. My friend ran to her, carried her in his arms, and told me, "Nabeel, this is my beloved daughter."

I started to weep, realizing from this picture how much God loves me. He loves me irrationally because He has the heart of the Father. This highest kind of love is what God has for us, and our ultimate calling is to grow to become like Him.

It is this fourth kind of love, irrational love, that God wants us to develop toward other young believers to help them grow. By investing ourselves in a young follower of Christ—using this book or other tools and methods to disciple him or her—we are developing a heart like the Father's.

In our Lebanon days, one of the key people in our ministry had a heart to serve God. I remember praying that God would provide him with an eager person who wanted to grow in Christ. God answered that prayer, and in the process my friend learned how to disciple people. Then I asked God to give him a very difficult person to disciple. I prayed this because God often uses difficult people to create a parent's heart within us. God answered that prayer too, and today that difficult person is a faithful servant of God in the Middle East.

When we belong to God's family, we start as children who are celebrating our new relationship with the Father. We then graduate from that stage when we realize we are not the center. Christ is the center, and we need to be fully surrendered to Him. That is the beginning of the discipleship stage, which will continue for the rest of our lives. This is as far as this book goes, yet we are called to an even higher relationship.

God desires for you to grow to full maturity, developing a *heart like His* so that you can reach out to others. In essence, this is growing in Christlikeness. Paul the apostle put it like this:

"And we, who with unveiled faces all reflect the Lord's glory, are being transformed into his likeness with ever-increasing glory, which comes from the Lord, who is the Spirit" (2 Corinthians 3:18).

What stage are you at, my friend? Are you ready to take the next step?

REFLECTION AND DISCUSSION QUESTIONS

1. Have you enjoyed a good "childhood" stage in your relationship with Christ? What things have you celebrated in this stage?
2. Have you moved into the discipleship stage? What helped you make that transition? What difference is it making in your life?
3. Do you have an opportunity to disciple someone else? Who would that be, and what steps would you take?

PART III

THE MANUAL:
GROWING IN CHRIST

Introduction
to the Manual

The following pages are a manual to help you develop two very important disciplines. The first involves meeting with God in the Word and prayer on a daily basis. This was a high value for Jesus. After a long, demanding day, He made this a priority. The Bible describes it this way: *"Very early in the morning, while it was still dark, Jesus got up, left the house and went off to a solitary place, where he prayed"* (Mark 1:35).

The second discipline is memorizing Scripture. Memorizing passages from the Bible—meditating on them and applying their truths to your life—will make a big difference in how you live on the moving walkway. I give you the same advice Moses gave to Joshua: *"Do not let this Book of the Law depart from your mouth; meditate on it day and night, so that you may be careful to do everything written in it. Then you will be prosperous and successful"* (Joshua 1:8).

These disciplines are like a two-edged sword. They can be a fantastic blessing, or they can become a curse of legalism. Please remember that *there is nothing you can do to make God love you more*. Reading the Bible, memorizing it, and praying do not add points with God. You do not need to try to earn His love and acceptance; you already have them.

Please also remember that *there is nothing you can do to make God love you less*. When you are not consistent in these disciplines, God is not shocked or disappointed. I do hope, my friend, that you are able to recognize and differentiate between the voices of the Holy Spirit, who is the Encourager, and the voice of the Devil, the accuser.

I look forward to traveling with you on the moving walkway as you use the manual that follows.

PART III

THE MANUAL:
GROWING IN CHRIST

THE FOLLOWING PAGES ARE DESIGNED TO HELP YOU KNOW GOD IN A deeper way. We will talk about reading the Bible, having a quiet time, memorizing Scripture, praying, and sharing your story with others. We'll start with quiet time, also known as devotional time. As you read, please always remember that just knowing the Bible is not our goal. Knowing God is our goal, and the Bible is the primary way we get to know Him.

I do hope, my friend, that as you spend time with Him each day in your *quiet time,* you will get to know Him more deeply. To help you begin this practice, this manual contains a passage from the Bible, followed by questions to think about and answer. Begin to do this day after day, and use these times to practice this spiritual discipline until it becomes a great habit in your life. Decide on a time and a place to spend uninterrupted time with God each day. My preference is to do it in the morning, although others choose the evening or over the lunch hour. Pick the time that will consistently work best for you.

If you make an appointment with someone important or special to you, you go to the meeting with anticipation. How much greater will that anticipation be as you prepare to meet with the almighty God! He wants to speak to you through the Bible, and He is eager to hear you speak back to Him through prayer.

During the first week, I will introduce another wonderful habit, *Scripture memory.* I am sure that you have memorized poems and religious texts in the past, so do not be intimidated by the idea of memorizing passages from the Bible. The benefits far outweigh the challenge.

During the third week, you will find suggestions on how to share with your friends and close relatives the proclamation *(da'wa).* Your friends and family members will listen to you to the degree they see positive transformation occurring in your life.

In the fourth week, you will learn to design your own quiet time using any part of the Bible.

I hope that the beginning of your new life in Christ has been a wonderful celebration. Please do continue to enjoy it as you move into a deeper relationship with Jesus and become His disciple. Permanent infancy is a disease; growth is essential. Remember always that your goal is knowing God, loving Him, and getting your life transformed so that you are more like Jesus.

Let us get going with the manual. May you be strong, firm, and steadfast (1 Peter 5:10–11) in your pursuit of Him.

QUIET TIME

If you don't want to write in this book, start a quiet-time notebook in which you record your answers to the questions and other thoughts.

FIRST WEEK

DAY 1   (DATE)

Spend a few minutes in prayer. Ask God to open your eyes so that you may see more of Him, and ask Him to nourish your soul through your time in His Word.

Read John 1:1–18 a couple of times.

Respond to the following questions.

1. Who is the "Word"? (*Logos* is the Greek word used here, which is translated as "Word." *Logos* was the name Greek philosophers gave to the Supreme Being. John used this important word, rooted in Jewish and Greek thinking, to talk about Jesus. Read verse 1 again replacing "*Logos*" with "Jesus," and see if it makes more sense.)

_____

_____

_____

2. Who is the light?

_____

_____

_____

3. In this text, what do you learn about the relationship of John the Baptist to Christ?

_____

_____

_____

4. What do you learn about Christ and how people responded to Him?

_____

_____

_____

5. What do verses 11–13 say to you and about you?

_____

_____

_____

6. What contrast do you see between Christ and Moses?

_____

_____

_____

Pray and thank God for what you have learned. Try to share something you learned with another follower of Christ today.

———◆•ﬓ•◆———

Day 2 _____ (DATE) _____

Spend a few moments in prayer. Ask God to speak to you through His Word.

Read John 1:19–34 a couple of times.

Respond to the following questions.

1. What was John the Baptist's purpose?

_____

_____

_____

_____

2. How did John the Baptist contrast himself to Christ?

_____

_____

_____

_____

3. Why did John the Baptist call Jesus the "Lamb of God"? What does "Lamb of God" mean? How is the term "Lamb of God" connected to Abraham and the Great Sacrifice (Al-Saffat Surah 37 verse 107)?

_____

_____

_____

_____

4. What do you learn about Christ in this text?

_____

_____

_____

_____

5. What else stood out to you in this text?

_____

_____

_____

Spend a few minutes in prayer, thanking God for His love and for what you have learned about Him today. Share with a friend some of your discoveries.

DAY 3   (DATE)

Spend a few moments in prayer. Ask God to speak to you through His Word.

Read John 1:35–51 a couple of times.

Respond to the following questions.

1. What was so appealing about Christ that made men leave their jobs to become His full-time disciples?

_____

_____

2. Why did John the Baptist encourage his own disciples to leave him and follow Jesus? What does that say about both John the Baptist and Jesus?

_____

_____

3. In the Middle East, people's names carry great significance. The name Peter means "rock." What do you think are the implications of Jesus changing Simon's name to Peter?

_____

_____

4. What was so appealing about the message that the disciples carried to one another: "We found the Messiah"?

_____

_____

5. What do you learn about Christ in this passage?

_____

_____

_____

Spend a few moments in prayer. Thank God for what you have learned and think about how you can follow Christ as His disciple throughout the day.

Scripture Memory

As part of today's quiet time, we will formally start with Scripture memory. This is a great tool to help you listen to God's truth instead of the Devil's accusations and lies.

Start today by memorizing John 5:24.

"'I tell you the truth, whoever hears my word and believes him who sent me has eternal life and will not be condemned; he has crossed over from death to life.'"

Practice by saying the reference before and after the verse. Repeat the reference with the first phrase in the verse many times until it sticks in your brain. (For example, *"John 5:24, I tell you the truth."*) Once you have memorized the first part, add another phrase. (*"John 5:24, I tell you the truth, whoever hears my word and believes him who sent me has eternal life."*) Then keep adding on until you have memorized the whole verse with the reference at both the beginning and end. There are two reasons for doing it this way. First, you will remember the reference when you quote the verse because you memorized it as part of the verse. Second, if the reference is mentioned, the first phrase of the verse will automatically come to your mind because you memorized them together.

Some people write the text they are memorizing on a card the size of a business card. I like to type them on a small piece of paper and laminate them.

More important than the way you memorize is your meditation and prayer over the contents of the verse. There is nothing spiritual about memorizing Bible verses. Even atheists can do that. What makes Scripture memory special and edifying is your meditation, prayer, and obedience to what you are memorizing. Delight in the Lord and His awesome promises as you are memorizing.

What follows is an example of the latest passage I have memorized in English (Philippians 2:5–11) and one of the lists I use to review verses I am memorizing. I like to review the verses during the "wasted" parts of my day, such as when I'm driving or waiting in line. I have the reference to each text followed by the first few words to help me remember. This is the method I like to use, but you should use whatever works best for you.

Philippians 2:5–11	1 Chron. 29:11 Yours, O Lord
Your attitude should be the same as	Ps. 57:1–2 Have mercy on me
that of Christ Jesus: Who, being in very	Matt. 11:28–30 Come to me,
nature God, did not consider equal-	Prov. 28:1, 13, 18 The wicked
ity with God something to be grasped	2 Cor. 4:16–18 Therefore we
but made himself nothing, taking the	Rom. 12:17–21 Do not repay
very nature of a servant, being made	Jude 1:24–25 To Him who is
in human likeness. And being found	Rom. 8:31–34 What, then
in appearance as a man, he humbled	Mark 7:20–23 What comes out
himself and became obedient to	Nahum 1:3, 7 The LORD is slow
death—even death on a cross! There-	1 Thess. 4:3–7 It is God's will
fore God exalted him to the highest	Isa. 54:7–8, 17 For a brief
place and gave him the name that is	Isa. 42:1 Here is my servant
above every name, that at the name of	Prov. 29:20–26 Do you see
Jesus every knee should bow, in heaven	Isa. 46:3–4 Listen to me
and on earth and under the earth, and	1 Pet. 4:7 The end of all
every tongue confess that Jesus Christ	Phil. 2:5–11 Your attitude
is Lord, to the glory of God the Father.	1 Chron. 4:9–10 Jabez was

Starting tomorrow, the fourth day, you will find a little box (☐) next to each day. Each day you review your verses, fill in this box until it becomes all black. Although I struggle sometimes to be faithful in memorizing Scripture, I find that this helps. May you take joy in seeing your boxes filled in!

———◆•※•◆———

☐ DAY 4   (DATE)

 Spend a few minutes in prayer. Ask God to speak to you through His Word.

Read John 2:1–25 a couple of times.

If you have them, find the maps in the back of your Bible. Become familiar with the places in Palestine. Jesus changed the water into wine in Cana in Galilee, and then He went to Capernaum, followed by Jerusalem. Do you see these towns on the map?

Respond to the following questions.

1. What events are mentioned in this chapter?

_____

_____

2. Consider the miracle of changing water into wine in light of what the Bible says about alcohol in Proverbs 23:29–32. What do you learn from this?

_____

_____

3. What do you learn about Jesus from this miracle?

_____

_____

4. What do you know about the Jewish Passover? (Read Exodus 12 to learn more about the historical roots of the Passover festival.)

_____

_____

5. What do you learn about Jesus from the incident at the temple? Why did He drive out the men who were selling cattle and sheep?

_____

_____

6. Isaiah 56:7 says, *"My house will be called a house of prayer for all nations."* How did the Jews treat the Gentiles, and what was the place of the Gentiles in the temple?

_____

_____

_____

7. What temple was Jesus talking about when He said that it would be destroyed and in three days it would be raised?

_____

_____

_____

8. Spend a few minutes thinking through what you read today. Did something from this chapter stand out to you and grip your heart? What thought can you carry through your day?

_____

_____

_____

☐ Day 5   (DATE)

Spend a few moments in prayer. Ask God to speak to you through His Word.

Read John 3:1–21 a couple of times.

Respond to the following questions.

1. How does this passage describe Nicodemus? Why did he come to Jesus at night?

_____

_____

_____

2. It only takes a few minutes to read this passage. How long do you think this conversation between Jesus and Nicodemus actually lasted? What were the issues, and how were they covered in the conversation?

_____

_____

_____

_____

3. What does being "born from above" mean? Can you explain how this happened to you?

_____

_____

_____

4. How would you explain verses 19–21, in light of what you see around you in the world?

_____

_____

_____

5. What especially stood out to you from this chapter? What thoughts can you take with you to think about and live out during the day?

_____

_____

_____

Have you reviewed John 5:24 and any other verses you are memorizing? Did you fill in the box?

---◆◆◆◆◆◆---

☐ DAY 6 _____ (DATE) _____

Spend a few moments in prayer. Ask God to speak to you through His Word.

Read John 3:22–36 a couple of times.

Respond to the following questions.

1. How did John the Baptist perceive himself as compared to Jesus?

_____

_____

_____

_____

2. What do you learn about Christ from this text?

_____

_____

3. In this text, we see that our attitude toward Christ will determine our destiny. Why is that?

_____

_____

4. In a practical way, how can you practice the phrase, "He must become greater; I must become less"? Spend some time praying over this verse, asking God what He wants you to be and to do.

_____

_____

Have you reviewed your verses today?

In Part II, I described the Devil as the "old landlord" who wants to plant seeds of doubt regarding your eternal security. He also comes to pour accusations and blame on you as soon as you fall into sin. He even tells you lies about God, like that He will never love you again because you treated Him with contempt or defiance. Do you remember the two truths? There is nothing you can do to make God love you more, and there is nothing you can do to make God love you less. Please memorize 1 John 1:9 and use it as frequently as needed.

"If we confess our sins, he is faithful and just and will forgive us our sins and purify us from all unrighteousness" (1 John 1:9).

Is there any unforgiven sin in your life? Remember, every single sin that you have committed has already been paid for by Jesus on the cross. Go to God and plead for forgiveness. Believe His promise that if you acknowledge and admit your sin and ask God for forgiveness—for breaking His heart—you are completely forgiven. You immediately will become completely clean from all defilement.

So far you have memorized at least two verses, John 5:24 and 1 John 1:9. Perhaps you are memorizing others as well. Continue to review these verses on a daily basis. When you have too many to review at one time, break them up into small groups. Remember to fill in the box every day after you have reviewed your verses.

☐ DAY 7 (DATE)

Spend a few moments in prayer. Ask God to speak to you through His Word.

Read John 4:1–42 a couple of times.

Respond to the following questions.

1. The person Jesus spoke with at the well was not only a Samaritan but a woman and a prostitute. What do you know about the relationship of the Jews and the Samaritans? What do you learn from Jesus' attitude toward the woman and how He talked with her?

_____

_____

_____

2. What do you learn about worship in this chapter?

_____

_____

_____

3. Practically speaking, how can you drink of the "Living Water" on a daily basis? What promises are given to you if you drink of that Water?

_____

_____

_____

4. What did the woman do in verses 28–30? What was the result?

_____

_____

_____

5. According to verse 42, why did Jesus visit our planet?

_____

_____

_____

_____

We see in this chapter, and in the Bible as a whole, that those who believed in Christ could not help but tell their friends and family about Jesus. Have you been telling others about your love for Jesus? In the process of being transformed into Christlikeness, the more you acknowledge Him, the faster you grow. Please remember that there is a good way and a bad way of acknowledging Jesus. The good way is to speak with humility and respect of your love and admiration for Jesus. The bad way is to leave people thinking you have committed high treason by adopting all the wrappings of Christianity and turning your back on your family and culture. Another bad way is to argue and attack the religion of the people you are talking to.

Ask God to give you boldness as you pray for some of your friends by name on a daily basis. You do not need to know a great deal about the Bible before you begin to speak. You are called to be a *witness,* not a *lawyer.* A lawyer is a highly educated expert, while a witness simply shares about what he or she has experienced. You can share honestly and with humility about how Christ is changing your life. Remember that the hero in your story is not you, but Christ. May you be like the woman Jesus met at the well, of whom it was said, *"We no longer believe just because of what you said; now we have heard for ourselves, and we know that this man really is the Savior of the world"* (John 4:42).

◆·◆·◆

SECOND WEEK

☐ Day 1   (DATE)
_____

 Spend a few moments in prayer. Ask God to speak to you through His Word.

Read John 4:43–54 a couple of times.

Respond to the following questions.

1. Please look at your map. In the text you just read, where was Jesus, and where had He previously been? What do you know about these places?

_____

_____

_____

2. What do you learn about Jesus and the types of people He related to?

_____

_____

_____

3. Why was it very important for the father to know the exact time his son was healed? (The Jewish day started at 6 A.M. The seventh hour means 1 P.M.)

_____

_____

_____

4. Do you think this father talked about Jesus? How do we know?

_____

_____

_____

5. The Greek word for household is *oikos*. How many people would you guess belonged to this man's household? Who would that household include?

_____

_____

_____

6. Are you struggling with an issue or a problem? Go to Jesus like this man did on behalf of his son.

_____

_____

_____

Although Jesus did not go to that particular town, people still believed in Him. Ask God to use you in your sphere of influence like He used that father. Spend a few minutes in prayer, asking God to pave the way for you with your friends.

☐ Day 2   (DATE)

Spend a few moments in prayer. Ask God to speak to you through His Word.

Read John 5:1–23 a couple of times.

Respond to the following questions.

1. How would you describe the situation of this sick man by the pool?

_____

_____

2. After Jesus healed the man, why did the Jews get angry? Are there people like that today, who cannot rejoice in the healing or saving of someone else (verse 18)? Why do you think they are like that?

_____

_____

3. What do we learn about Jesus and His Father from John 5:19–23?

_____

_____

4. What is Jesus' role on the Day of Judgment, according to verse 22?

_____

_____

_____

Spend a few minutes in prayer, thanking God for what you learned today. Ask Him to help you meditate on one specific truth from this chapter. You might want to write it down and meditate on it throughout the day.

 Memorize 1 Corinthians 10:13.

"No temptation has seized you except what is common to man. And God is faithful; he will not let you be tempted beyond what you can bear. But when you are tempted, he will also provide a way out so that you can stand up under it."

Trust God and His promise. Ask Him for a way out. That might mean telling a brother or sister in Christ about your temptation or staying away from circumstances that cause the temptation. Remember, my friend, God wants to purify us and make us like pure gold!

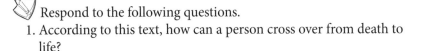

☐ Day 3   (DATE)

Spend a few moments in prayer. Ask God to speak to you through His Word.

Read John 5:24–47 a couple of times.

Respond to the following questions.

1. According to this text, how can a person cross over from death to life?

2. In Daniel 7:13–14, the prophet Daniel had this vision about the "Son of Man": *"'In my vision at night I looked, and there before me was one like a son of man, coming with the clouds of heaven. He approached the Ancient of Days [God] and was led into his presence. He was given authority, glory and sovereign power; all peoples, nations and men of every language worshiped him. His dominion is an everlasting dominion that will not pass away, and his kingdom is one that will never be destroyed.'"*

What did Jesus mean when He called Himself the Son of Man in John 5:27?

_____

_____

3. When Stephen was martyred, he had a vision of God, which is described in Acts 7:54–58. He said: *"I see heaven open and the Son of Man standing at the right hand of God."* Stephen was quoting Daniel 7 as he spoke of Jesus. What do you think Steven understood from the title "Son of Man"?

_____

_____

4. Who and what give testimony about Jesus' authenticity? How?

_____

_____

5. What stood out to you from this text? What ideas can you think about throughout the day?

_____

_____

_____

_____

_____

☐ Day 4 _____ (DATE)

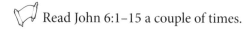 Spend a few moments in prayer. Ask God to speak to you through His Word.

Read John 6:1–15 a couple of times.

Respond to the following questions.

1. Look at the map in your Bible and locate where this miracle took place. Is there any significance about this place?

_____

_____

_____

2. If you were one of the disciples who witnessed this miracle, what impact would it have made on you?

_____

_____

_____

3. What types of people witnessed this miracle? Why did they follow Jesus?

_____

_____

_____

4. Is it significant that 12 baskets of food were left over? Can you think of what the number 12 might signify?

_____

_____

_____

5. Are you more like Philip or more like Andrew in how you address challenges (verses 7 and 8)?

_____

_____

_____

6. In light of what you read today, what areas of your life do you need to talk to God about?

_____

_____

_____

☐ Day 5   (DATE)

Spend a few moments in prayer. Ask God to speak to you through His Word.

Read John 6:16–40 a couple of times.

Respond to the following questions.

1. Using your Bible map, find where these incidents took place.

2. When God talked to Moses from the burning bush (Exodus 3:14), God called Himself "*I am who I am.*" What did Jesus call Himself as He walked on the water toward the disciples? Why is this significant?

_____

_____

_____

3. What is the significance of the conversation Jesus had with the Jews about bread and manna?

_____

_____

_____

4. What does Jesus say about Himself in this text?

_____

_____

_____

5. Give some reasons why people today seek Jesus. Are they similar to the motives of those we see in this chapter?

_____

_____

_____

6. How can you practically feed yourself today on the "bread from heaven"?

_____

_____

_____

Today, memorize Romans 8:32.

"He who did not spare his own Son, but gave him up for us all—how will he not also, along with him, graciously give us all things?"

If you are more ambitious, try memorizing Romans 8:31–34. As you memorize, enjoy deep intimacy with God, who loves you and gave you these promises. Hold tight to them and trust Him every day as you meditate on His Word.

☐ Day 6 (DATE)

Spend a few moments in prayer. Ask God to speak to you through His Word.

Read John 6:41–71 a couple of times.

Respond to the following questions.

1. What do you learn about Christ from this text?

_____

_____

_____

2. During their 40 years in the wilderness, the Israelites survived on the manna that God provided (Exodus 16). What are the similarities between the manna and Jesus, the Bread of Life? What are the differences?

_____

_____

_____

3. Practically speaking, how can you abide in Christ on a daily basis?

_____

_____

_____

_____

_____

4. Why did Peter and the disciples continue to follow Jesus? Have you found it hard at times to continue following Jesus? Why? What motivates you to continue?

_____

_____

_____

_____

5. Are there people today who are abandoning Jesus? Why?

_____

_____

_____

_____

Spend some time in prayer. Affirm your commitment to Christ, and tell Him why you want to follow Him the rest of your life.

———◆•✷•◆———

☐ DAY 7 _____   (DATE)

Spend a few moments in prayer. Ask God to speak to you through His Word.

Read John 7:1–27 a couple of times.

Respond to the following questions.
1. This chapter is set during the Feast of Tabernacles. What do you know about this event?[1]

_____

_____

_____

---

1 I recommend a free program you can download from the Internet at www.e-sword.net. The commentaries and dictionaries of this Bible program helped me understand the historical background of difficult texts as well as many other things. The program uses various translations, including one in Arabic.

2. According to John 7:17, what are the conditions for getting to
   know Christ?

   _____

   _____

   _____

3. According to the text, why did the Jews want to kill Jesus?

   _____

   _____

   _____

4. In what ways did Jesus differ from the Jews in His understanding
   of the Sabbath?

   _____

   _____

   _____

   _____

5. What can you take from this text to think and meditate on during
   your day?

   _____

   _____

   _____

PRAYER

One of the verses you have memorized is Romans 8:32: *"He who did not
spare his own Son, but gave him up for us all—how will he not also, along
with him, graciously give us all things?"*

God wants to lavish His grace upon us. One of the ways to tap into
His abundant grace is to talk to Him in prayer.

Mark 1:35 describes how Jesus, after a long, exhausting day, got up
early the next morning to spend time with God in prayer.

*"Very early in the morning, while it was still dark, Jesus got up, left the
house and went off to a solitary place, where he prayed."*

Prayer can take a number of forms, but a helpful way to start is to
use the ACTS principle: **A**doration, **C**onfession, **T**hanksgiving, and
Supplication.

Adoration and praise. The Psalms *(Zabour)* are one of the best places to learn how to praise God for His qualities of excellence. The psalmist suggests that we enter into the presence of God with praise and thanksgiving: *"Enter his gates with thanksgiving and his courts with praise; give thanks to him and praise his name"* (Psalm 100:4).

One time I was asked by a friend to have our quiet times together. We got our Bibles and started going up the stairs to the third floor where his office was. As we went up the stairs, his voice got more and more quiet until it felt like we were entering a place of worship. I do not remember if we knelt down or sat on chairs, but reverently he started apologizing to God. He prayed: "Forgive us, Lord, for rushing into Your presence." His prayer reminded me that at that very moment, I was in the very presence of His Majesty, the King of kings and Lord of lords, and it was appropriate to praise Him.

Sometimes, I like to start out by using the words of David in 1 Chronicles 29:11: *"Yours, O LORD, is the greatness and the power and the glory and the majesty and the splendor, for everything in heaven and earth is yours. Yours, O LORD, is the kingdom; you are exalted as head over all."* Having memorized this text helps me at times in starting my prayer with it.

Confession. We have memorized 1 John 1:9: *"If we confess our sins, he is faithful and just and will forgive us our sins and purify us from all unrighteousness."* Falling into sin is like the toddler falling down on the moving walkway. When we confess, it is like that toddler hearing the voice of his dad, getting up from his fall, and resuming his walk toward his father who loves him.

Do not let one sin rob you of your joy and deep intimacy with the Father. Do not live with defilement and shame when you can be pure and clean. King David wrote one of the most beautiful psalms after he repented of his sins of adultery and murder. Psalm 51 is worth memorizing and using in your prayer of confession. (You can use the page in Appendix 2 of this book to add references you want to memorize in the future.)

Thanksgiving. When we thank God and accept our circumstances, we tune into His wavelength. We become aware that He is in full control of current events in the world and our lives. The apostle Paul told the Thessalonians to *"give thanks in all circumstances, for this is God's will for you in Christ Jesus"* (1 Thessalonians 5:18). One of the big keys to having contentment and joy is to practice this truth.

Giving thanks is more than what we do during our quiet times. It is an attitude we carry throughout the day.

Supplication. Pray for your needs and the needs of others. Remember these words of Jesus: *"Ask and it will be given to you; seek and you will find; knock and the door will be opened to you. For everyone who asks receives; he who seeks finds; and to him who knocks, the door will be opened. Which of you, if his son asks for bread, will give him a stone? Or if he asks for a fish, will give him a snake? If you, then, though you are evil, know how to give good gifts to your children, how much more will your Father in heaven give good gifts to those who ask him!"* (Matthew 7:7–11).

Jabez, one of God's men in the Old Testament, prayed this prayer: *"'Oh, that you would bless me and enlarge my territory! Let your hand be with me, and keep me from harm so that I will be free from pain'"* (1 Chronicles 4:10). In another translation, the last sentence says, *"That I may not cause pain to myself and others."*

The Bible tells us that God answered this prayer. This short prayer is worth memorizing and praying on a regular basis.

Supplication also involves praying for other people. The apostle Paul asked the Ephesians to pray for God's people. *"Pray in the Spirit on all occasions with all kinds of prayers and requests. With this in mind, be alert and always keep on praying for all the saints"* (Ephesians 6:18). Belonging to God's family assumes the responsibilities of love, care, and prayer for God's people.

Consider the prayer that Jesus taught to His disciples in Matthew 6. What elements of the ACTS principle do you see in it?

"'Our Father in heaven, hallowed be your name, your kingdom come, your will be done on earth as it is in heaven. Give us today our daily bread. Forgive us our debts, as we also have forgiven our debtors. And lead us not into temptation, but deliver us from the evil one'" (Matthew 6:9–13).

When you pray, try to remember ACTS—Adoration, Confession, Thanksgiving, and Supplication. This will keep your prayers balanced and complete.

THIRD WEEK

☐ Day 1   (DATE)

Spend a few moments in prayer. Ask God to speak to you through His Word.

Read John 7:28–53 a couple of times.

Respond to the following questions.

1. How does Jesus allude to the coming crucifixion in this text?

_____

_____

_____

2. During the Feast of Tabernacles, the priest poured water on the altar. Jesus stood in a prominent place in the temple and cried out, *"If anyone is thirsty, let him come to me and drink"* (verse 37). What do you think of this invitation?

_____

_____

_____

3. Various people perceived Jesus differently. Why?

_____

_____

_____

4. How do different kinds of people perceive Jesus today? Why the differences?

_____

_____

_____

5. How can you come to Christ throughout the day and drink of the "living water"?

_____

_____

_____

_____

6. What can you share with others—and how can you share it—about what you are learning during your quiet times? How can you share about Jesus without "the wrappings"?

_____

_____

_____

Memorize Jeremiah 15:16.

*"When your words came, I ate them; they were my joy and my heart's delight, for I bear your name, O L*ORD *God Almighty."*

This verse promises joy and delight to those who "eat" the Word of God. This means reading it, studying it, and meditating on it.

Take a quick look at your quiet time record. Have you been "eating" the Word? Have you been filling in the boxes as you review your verses?

☐ DAY 2   (DATE)

Spend a few moments in prayer. Ask God to speak to you through His Word.

Read John 8:1–20 a couple of times.

Respond to the following questions.

1. The first 11 verses tell the story of a woman caught in adultery. Why were some people so judgmental of this woman?

_____

_____

2. Why are people judgmental today?

_____

_____

_____

3. Christ was the only one who was without sin, the only one with the right to stone her. Why was He merciful? Do you think of God more like Christ or more like the judgmental Pharisees?

_____

_____

_____

4. What did Jesus say about His relationship with the Father?

_____

_____

_____

5. How can we daily, and in practical ways, walk in the light as we follow Jesus, the Light of the World (verse 12)?

_____

_____

_____

_____

_____

_____

☐ Day 3   (DATE) _____

Spend a few moments in prayer. Ask God to speak to you through His Word.

Read John 8:21–47 a couple of times.

Respond to the following questions.
1. What do you learn about Christ from this text?

_____

_____

_____

2. What did Jesus mean by "truth" (verse 32)? We lose our freedom when we believe lies about God and ourselves. How can truth set us free? Can you think of practical illustrations?

---

3. According to verse 35, what is the difference between a slave and a son? How permanent is the relationship between a father and his children compared to his relationships with his employees?

---

4. What do you learn about the Devil from verse 44? How does the Devil use people?

---

5. Have you experienced persecution? Was it because of your faith in Christ or because of the wrong ways you acknowledged Christ?

---

6. According to Philippians 1:29, what should your attitude be when you are persecuted for the right reasons?

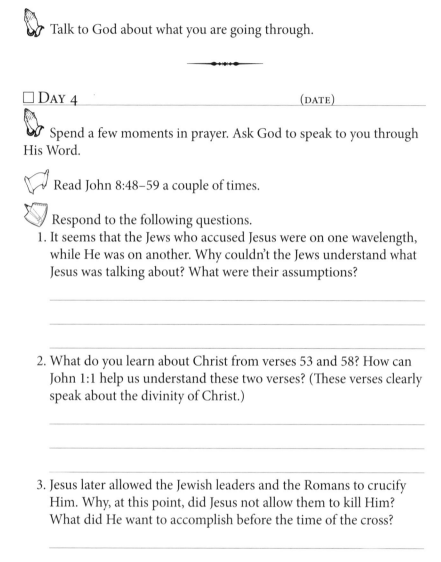

Talk to God about what you are going through.

———◆—▷◁◆◁—◆———

☐ DAY 4   (DATE)

Spend a few moments in prayer. Ask God to speak to you through His Word.

Read John 8:48–59 a couple of times.

Respond to the following questions.

1. It seems that the Jews who accused Jesus were on one wavelength, while He was on another. Why couldn't the Jews understand what Jesus was talking about? What were their assumptions?

_____

_____

2. What do you learn about Christ from verses 53 and 58? How can John 1:1 help us understand these two verses? (These verses clearly speak about the divinity of Christ.)

_____

_____

3. Jesus later allowed the Jewish leaders and the Romans to crucify Him. Why, at this point, did Jesus not allow them to kill Him? What did He want to accomplish before the time of the cross?

_____

_____

Spend some time in prayer, adoring Him, confessing your sins to Him, thanking Him, and making requests for yourself and others. One of the ways to develop your praise and worship is by singing hymns. Learn some hymns, or even write your own poems or hymns of praise to God.

☐ Day 5   (DATE)

Spend a few moments in prayer. Ask God to speak to you through His Word.

Read John 9:1–41 a couple of times.

Respond to the following questions.

1. What explains the diversity of responses among the neighbors, the Pharisees, and the parents of the formerly blind man?

---

2. What were the circumstances of the blind man that prepared him to believe in Christ?

---

3. How did his faith in Christ evolve?

---

4. What misconceptions did the disciples have (verse 2)? What is the truth?

---

5. What misconceptions did the Jews have about God (verses 31–34)? Do these misconceptions continue today?

_____

_____

_____

6. Do you identify with this blind man in how you came to believe in Christ? How? Does verse 39 apply to your situation now or in the past?

_____

_____

_____

Spend some time in prayer thanking God and praying for friends and relatives who continue to suffer from spiritual blindness.

SHARING YOUR STORY

Have you had opportunities to talk about what Christ has done in your life to your friends and relatives? When the blind man was asked what happened to him, he said: *"One thing I do know. I was blind but now I see!"* (John 9:25). He did not know theology or doctrine, but he knew his life was transformed, and he boldly spoke about it. Do not wait until you know more of the Bible before you speak out. If your life is being transformed, tell people about it. Share with your friends what Jesus has been doing in your life. Remember that the power of your words will come from the evidence of a transformed life.

It will help if you write your story in one page so that you can share it in two to four minutes. You can follow this outline:

1. What was your life like before you surrendered it to Christ?
2. Describe your journey toward Christ.
3. Describe some of your struggles and how you finally surrendered your life to Christ and believed in Him.
4. What is your life like now, and what changes has Christ made in you so far?
   - The contrast does not have to focus on how you were "bad" before and now you are better. The contrast could be between a life with no purpose and a life that now has purpose and meaning.

- Refer to actual events that could be meaningful to your friends. Try to help them identify with what you are saying.
- Avoid long, boring stories or events.
- Remember that the hero of your story is not you, but Jesus.
- Remember that your story is merely an introduction to the facts of the Gospel. The story of the apostle Paul in Acts 26 could be a good guide as you write your story.
- Read your story to a friend who is a follower of Christ and understands your background. Ask your friend to help you improve it.

☐ Day 6   (DATE)

Spend a few moments in prayer. Ask God to speak to you through His Word.

Read John 10:1–30 a couple of times.

Respond to the following questions.
1. What did Christ say about Himself in this text?

_____

_____

_____

_____

_____

_____

2. Intelligence is not the key in recognizing Christ. It takes something else. What is this, according to verses 22–30?

_____

_____

_____

_____

3. What does Jesus say about you in this text?

_____

_____

_____

Spend some time in prayer and thanksgiving over what you have learned about Christ and yourself in this chapter. Ask God to help you know what to share with your unbelieving friends. What verses would appeal to your friends and family?

Memorize John 10:27–29.

"'My sheep listen to my voice; I know them, and they follow me. I give them eternal life, and they shall never perish; no one can snatch them out of my hand. My Father, who has given them to me, is greater than all; no one can snatch them out of my Father's hand.'"

———◆◆◆◆———

☐ Day 7   (DATE)

Spend a few moments in prayer. Ask God to speak to you through His Word.

Read John 10:31–42 a couple of times.

Respond to the following questions.

1. Why did the Jews want to stone Christ to death? Were their accusations accurate? What was the truth?

_____

_____

_____

2. What did Christ say about Himself in this text?

_____

_____

_____

_____

3. If Jesus came to our planet today with the same teachings and lifestyle, how would people respond to Him?

_____

_____

_____

4. How can you help your friends and family have a better understanding of Jesus?

_____

_____

_____

Spend a few moments in prayer for yourself and your family and friends. Ask God to open their eyes to recognize Jesus.

Scripture Memory: How are you doing? Write down, from memory, the references and words of all the verses you have memorized so far. (You could also ask someone to check you while you say the verses aloud.) This will be a good way to find out if you have made any mistakes in your memorizing.

Developing Your Own Quiet Time

For the past three weeks, I have given you the text to read and questions to help you think through what you read. This week, you will start a new stage in your quiet time. Now you will have more responsibility for learning to "chew and digest" God's Word on your own. Remember that your goal is to have an "appointment" with the almighty God on a daily basis.

Over the years, I have tried several methods of having a quiet time with God. The following suggestions are the most practical method I have found. I do hope and pray, my friend, that your quiet time will surpass what I do. I pray it will become a daily highlight that you long for and enjoy.

1. Start with prayer, remembering that you are in the presence of His Majesty, the King of kings and Lord of lords. Listen to God say to you, *"Be still, and know that I am God"* (Psalm 46:10).
2. Read part of a chapter or a whole chapter at one time. I recommend that you stay in one book of the Bible until you complete it instead of jumping around. As you read, expect the Holy Spirit

to open your eyes so you will see what He wants to reveal to you. *"The unfolding of your words gives light; it gives understanding. . . "* (Psalm 119:130).

3. Go back and focus on what stood out to you most and meditate on it. Focus on one verse or one idea. Use categories like these to write your discoveries. (In Appendix 4 of this book, you will find pages you can photocopy and make into a booklet that becomes a journal for your time with God.)

Sunday   Date: _____   All I read today: _____

Best thing I marked today (reference): _____

Thought: _____

How it impressed me: _____

4. Your accuracy in understanding what the Bible says will make your quiet time more valuable. Pay attention to the context of the verse or text. What does the text mean in its context? Are there other texts or cross-references that can help you better understand what you read? What do you learn about Jesus? Is there a command you need to obey? Is there a promise you can claim?

5. Write down what impressed you from the passage. Measure yourself by the standard of His Word. Be honest and transparent before God, and make some applications if God speaks to you.

6. If you do not have time to write much, write one sentence about your thoughts and discoveries. Then write a short prayer about how it impressed you. Being brief may help you be consistent.

Some people find it hard to write during their quiet times. It reminds them of homework and feels rigid and boring. But others look at their writing as a daily journal and a record of their interaction with God. If you start and persevere for a while, you might enjoy it. Remember that you will not add points with God by having a quiet time. He already loves you with perfect love. All you are doing is responding to His love by spending meaningful time with Him.

In the coming weeks and months, get into this "discipline of grace." Even if you find it difficult in the beginning, persevere. In a long race, many people start, but few persevere to the end. This may become one of the greatest habits of your life.

Keep going, my friend.

It is time now for me to end my journey with you. I thank you for walking with me through the pages of this book. I pray that you have been encouraged, challenged, and, most of all, liberated from your life of futile striving on the descending escalator. What God wants from you is to live freely and joyfully on the moving walkway, to get to know Him better, and to trust your life to Him. I have tried to get you off to a good start through this book. Now it is up to you to find other resources—books and materials (see my recommended list in Appendix 7) and the fellowship of other believers—to help you grow. I pray, my friend, that you will continue growing. And please feel free to contact me by e-mail at drjabbour@nabeeljabbour.com.

"[Be] confident of this, that he who began a good work in you will carry it on to completion until the day of Christ Jesus" (Philippians 1:6).

APPENDICES

THE SERMON
ON THE MOUNT

IN CHAPTER 6, I TALKED ABOUT THE SERMON ON THE MOUNT AND how it gives us a good look at the intent and heart of the law. I believe understanding this is so important that I have included the entire text of the sermon here. You will see that Christ affirms the law, but He also gives a great invitation to surpass it, to go behind it, and to look at God's absolute standards and His heart.

During Christ's visit to our planet, at a time when He was surrounded by crowds, He went up on a mountainside alone and sat down. His disciples came closer to Him, so He began to teach them while the crowds listened in. These people had the amazing privilege to learn the very secrets of God as Jesus revealed what is behind that thick "curtain" that separated humanity from God. By reading the Sermon on the Mount, contained here in its entirety, we have that same privilege.

A PEAK BEHIND THE LAW

In Matthew 5, Jesus said: ³"Blessed are the poor in spirit, for theirs is the kingdom of heaven. ⁴Blessed are those who mourn, for they will be comforted. ⁵Blessed are the meek, for they will inherit the earth. ⁶Blessed are those who hunger and thirst for righteousness, for they will be filled. ⁷Blessed are the merciful, for they will be shown mercy. ⁸Blessed are the pure in heart, for they will see God. ⁹Blessed are the peacemakers, for they will be called sons of God. ¹⁰Blessed are those who are persecuted because of righteousness, for theirs is the kingdom of heaven. ¹¹"Blessed are you when people insult you, persecute you and falsely say all kinds of evil against you because of me. ¹²Rejoice and be glad, because great is your reward in heaven, for in the same way they persecuted the prophets who were before you.

¹³"You are the salt of the earth. But if the salt loses its saltiness, how

can it be made salty again? It is no longer good for anything, except to be thrown out and trampled by men. [14]You are the light of the world. A city on a hill cannot be hidden. [15]Neither do people light a lamp and put it under a bowl. Instead they put it on its stand, and it gives light to everyone in the house. [16]In the same way, let your light shine before men, that they may see your good deeds and praise your Father in heaven.

[17]"Do not think that I have come to abolish the Law or the Prophets; I have not come to abolish them but to fulfill them. [18]I tell you the truth, until heaven and earth disappear, not the smallest letter, not the least stroke of a pen, will by any means disappear from the Law until everything is accomplished. [19]Anyone who breaks one of the least of these commandments and teaches others to do the same will be called least in the kingdom of heaven, but whoever practices and teaches these commands will be called great in the kingdom of heaven. [20]For I tell you that unless your righteousness surpasses that of the Pharisees and the teachers of the law, you will certainly not enter the kingdom of heaven.

[21]"You have heard that it was said to the people long ago, 'Do not murder, and anyone who murders will be subject to judgment.' [22]But I tell you that anyone who is angry with his brother will be subject to judgment. Again, anyone who says to his brother, 'Raca,' is answerable to the Sanhedrin. But anyone who says, 'You fool!' will be in danger of the fire of hell.

[23]"Therefore, if you are offering your gift at the altar and there remember that your brother has something against you, [24]leave your gift there in front of the altar. First go and be reconciled to your brother; then come and offer your gift.

[25]"Settle matters quickly with your adversary who is taking you to court. Do it while you are still with him on the way, or he may hand you over to the judge, and the judge may hand you over to the officer, and you may be thrown into prison. [26]I tell you the truth, you will not get out until you have paid the last penny.

[27]"You have heard that it was said, 'Do not commit adultery.' [28]But I tell you that anyone who looks at a woman lustfully has already committed adultery with her in his heart. [29]If your right eye causes you to sin, gouge it out and throw it away. It is better for you to lose one part of your body than for your whole body to be thrown into hell. [30]And if your right hand causes you to sin, cut it off and throw it away. It is better for you to lose one part of your body than for your whole body to go into hell.

[31]"It has been said, 'Anyone who divorces his wife must give her a certificate of divorce.' [32]But I tell you that anyone who divorces his wife,

except for marital unfaithfulness, causes her to become an adulteress, and anyone who marries the divorced woman commits adultery.

[33]"Again, you have heard that it was said to the people long ago, 'Do not break your oath, but keep the oaths you have made to the Lord.' [34]But I tell you, Do not swear at all: either by heaven, for it is God's throne; [35]or by the earth, for it is his footstool; or by Jerusalem, for it is the city of the Great King. [36]And do not swear by your head, for you cannot make even one hair white or black. [37]Simply let your 'Yes' be 'Yes,' and your 'No,' 'No'; anything beyond this comes from the evil one.

[38]"You have heard that it was said, 'Eye for eye, and tooth for tooth.' [39]But I tell you, Do not resist an evil person. If someone strikes you on the right cheek, turn to him the other also. [40]And if someone wants to sue you and take your tunic, let him have your cloak as well. [41]If someone forces you to go one mile, go with him two miles. [42]Give to the one who asks you, and do not turn away from the one who wants to borrow from you.

[43]"You have heard that it was said, 'Love your neighbor and hate your enemy.' [44]But I tell you: Love your enemies and pray for those who persecute you, [45]that you may be sons of your Father in heaven. He causes his sun to rise on the evil and the good, and sends rain on the righteous and the unrighteous. [46]If you love those who love you, what reward will you get? Are not even the tax collectors doing that? [47]And if you greet only your brothers, what are you doing more than others? Do not even pagans do that? [48]Be perfect, therefore, as your heavenly Father is perfect."

Chapter 6

[1]"Be careful not to do your 'acts of righteousness' before men, to be seen by them. If you do, you will have no reward from your Father in heaven. [2]So when you give to the needy, do not announce it with trumpets, as the hypocrites do in the synagogues and on the streets, to be honored by men. I tell you the truth, they have received their reward in full. [3]But when you give to the needy, do not let your left hand know what your right hand is doing, [4]so that your giving may be in secret. Then your Father, who sees what is done in secret, will reward you.

[5]"And when you pray, do not be like the hypocrites, for they love to pray standing in the synagogues and on the street corners to be seen by men. I tell you the truth, they have received their reward in full. [6]But when you pray, go into your room, close the door and pray to your Father, who is unseen. Then your Father, who sees what is done in secret, will reward you. [7]And when you pray, do not keep on babbling like pagans, for they think they will be heard because of their many words.

[8]Do not be like them, for your Father knows what you need before you ask him.

[9]"This, then, is how you should pray: 'Our Father in heaven, hallowed be your name, [10]your kingdom come, your will be done on earth as it is in heaven. [11]Give us today our daily bread. [12]Forgive us our debts, as we also have forgiven our debtors. [13]And lead us not into temptation, but deliver us from the evil one.'

[14]For if you forgive men when they sin against you, your heavenly Father will also forgive you. [15]But if you do not forgive men their sins, your Father will not forgive your sins.

[16]"When you fast, do not look somber as the hypocrites do, for they disfigure their faces to show men they are fasting. I tell you the truth, they have received their reward in full. [17]But when you fast, put oil on your head and wash your face, [18]so that it will not be obvious to men that you are fasting, but only to your Father, who is unseen; and your Father, who sees what is done in secret, will reward you.

[19]"Do not store up for yourselves treasures on earth, where moth and rust destroy, and where thieves break in and steal. [20]But store up for yourselves treasures in heaven, where moth and rust do not destroy, and where thieves do not break in and steal. [21]For where your treasure is, there your heart will be also.

[22]"The eye is the lamp of the body. If your eyes are good, your whole body will be full of light. [23]But if your eyes are bad, your whole body will be full of darkness. If then the light within you is darkness, how great is that darkness!

[24]"No one can serve two masters. Either he will hate the one and love the other, or he will be devoted to the one and despise the other. You cannot serve both God and Money.

[25]"Therefore I tell you, do not worry about your life, what you will eat or drink; or about your body, what you will wear. Is not life more important than food, and the body more important than clothes? [26]Look at the birds of the air; they do not sow or reap or store away in barns, and yet your heavenly Father feeds them. Are you not much more valuable than they? [27]Who of you by worrying can add a single hour to his life?

[28]"And why do you worry about clothes? See how the lilies of the field grow. They do not labor or spin. [29]Yet I tell you that not even Solomon in all his splendor was dressed like one of these. [30]If that is how God clothes the grass of the field, which is here today and tomorrow is thrown into the fire, will he not much more clothe you, O you of little faith? [31]So

do not worry, saying, 'What shall we eat?' or 'What shall we drink?' or 'What shall we wear?' [32]For the pagans run after all these things, and your heavenly Father knows that you need them. [33]But seek first his kingdom and his righteousness, and all these things will be given to you as well. [34]Therefore do not worry about tomorrow, for tomorrow will worry about itself. Each day has enough trouble of its own."

Chapter 7

[1]"Do not judge, or you too will be judged. [2]For in the same way you judge others, you will be judged, and with the measure you use, it will be measured to you. [3]Why do you look at the speck of sawdust in your brother's eye and pay no attention to the plank in your own eye? [4]How can you say to your brother, 'Let me take the speck out of your eye,' when all the time there is a plank in your own eye? [5]You hypocrite, first take the plank out of your own eye, and then you will see clearly to remove the speck from your brother's eye.

[6]"Do not give dogs what is sacred; do not throw your pearls to pigs. If you do, they may trample them under their feet, and then turn and tear you to pieces.

[7]"Ask and it will be given to you; seek and you will find; knock and the door will be opened to you. [8]For everyone who asks receives; he who seeks finds; and to him who knocks, the door will be opened.

[9]"Which of you, if his son asks for bread, will give him a stone? [10]Or if he asks for a fish, will give him a snake? [11]If you, then, though you are evil, know how to give good gifts to your children, how much more will your Father in heaven give good gifts to those who ask him! [12]So in everything, do to others what you would have them do to you, for this sums up the Law and the Prophets.

[13]"Enter through the narrow gate. For wide is the gate and broad is the road that leads to destruction, and many enter through it. [14]But small is the gate and narrow the road that leads to life, and only a few find it.

[15]"Watch out for false prophets. They come to you in sheep's clothing, but inwardly they are ferocious wolves. [16]By their fruit you will recognize them. Do people pick grapes from thornbushes, or figs from thistles? [17]Likewise every good tree bears good fruit, but a bad tree bears bad fruit. [18]A good tree cannot bear bad fruit, and a bad tree cannot bear good fruit. [19]Every tree that does not bear good fruit is cut down and thrown into the fire. [20]Thus, by their fruit you will recognize them.

[21]"Not everyone who says to me, 'Lord, Lord,' will enter the kingdom of heaven, but only he who does the will of my Father who is in heaven.

²²Many will say to me on that day, 'Lord, Lord, did we not prophesy in your name, and in your name drive out demons and perform many miracles?' ²³Then I will tell them plainly, 'I never knew you. Away from me, you evildoers!'

²⁴"Therefore everyone who hears these words of mine and puts them into practice is like a wise man who built his house on the rock. ²⁵The rain came down, the streams rose, and the winds blew and beat against that house; yet it did not fall, because it had its foundation on the rock. ²⁶But everyone who hears these words of mine and does not put them into practice is like a foolish man who built his house on sand. ²⁷The rain came down, the streams rose, and the winds blew and beat against that house, and it fell with a great crash."

Reflection and Discussion Questions

1. What did you discover? What impressed you or stood out to you?
2. In Matthew 5:17–20, Jesus talks about the law. How did He surpass the law?
3. In Matthew 5:21–22 and 27–30, Jesus spoke about God's absolute standards behind the law. How can these standards serve as a mirror that shows our true selves?
4. In Matthew 5:38–48, Jesus goes beyond the Jewish law to the heart of God. How does this teaching surpass any and every law in the world today?
5. What do you learn from Matthew 6:1–8 and 16–18 about appearances versus reality?
6. From Matthew 6:28–34, what do you learn about God and His love for you? What do you learn about the value of worrying?
7. Who has the right to judge others and why (Matthew 7:1–5)?
8. According to Matthew 7:7–12, what is God like? Is He like a mean teacher who wants to punish you for every mistake you make?
9. Who is able to enter the kingdom of God (Matthew 7:13–23)?
10. If the passing grade is nothing less than 100 percent, what is the solution?

SCRIPTURE

MEMORY VERSES

WHILE GOING THROUGH PART III OF THIS BOOK, YOU HAVE MEMORIZED the following verses:

A new creation	John 5:24
Assurance of forgiveness	1 John 1:9
Assurance of victory	1 Corinthians 10:13
Assurance of God's care	Romans 8:32
The Word	Jeremiah 15:16
The love of God	John 10:27–29

The topics I have included here are part of the Topical Memory System,[1] but I have chosen to use different verses. After you finish this book, you may want to get a copy of the Topical Memory System to learn more verses on each subject. This plan includes important topics that can help you on your journey in a life of discipleship. There are 30 topics, and every 6 topics form an independent unit. You can add more verses to these topics as you read and as God speaks to you. There are spaces for the additional verses that you might choose to memorize in the future.

It is not so important how many verses you memorize, but how the Holy Spirit is using these verses in your life. If you find that in your quiet time or in your Scripture memory you are slipping into a legalistic mode of trying to earn God's acceptance, then stop for a while. Correct your motives, then continue and persevere.

---

1 The Topical Memory System is available from NavPress: www.navpress.com or (800) 366-7788.

The New Life

Christ the Center

    John 15:4

Obedience to Christ

    Matthew 12:50

The Word

    Psalm 119:105

Prayer

    Lamentations 2:19

Fellowship

    Proverbs 27:17

Witness

    John 15:16

Proclaim Christ

Holiness of God

    1 Peter 1:15–16

Lostness of Man

    Isaiah 59:2

Destiny of the Lost

    John 3:36

God's Deliverance

    Romans 5:10

Grace of God

    Romans 3:24

Man's Responsibility

    John 3:3

Rely on God's Resources

His Spirit

John 14:26

His Strength

Ezekiel 3:8–9

His Faithfulness

Isaiah 49:15–16

His Peace

John 14:27

His Provision

Matthew 10:29–30

His Help in Temptation

James 4:7

Be Christ's Disciple

Put Christ First

John 6:68–69

Separation

John 17:15–16

Steadfastness

Habakkuk 3:17–18

Serving

Isaiah 58:10–11

Giving

Deuteronomy 15:10–11

Vision

Luke 24:47

CHRISTLIKENESS

Love

  1 Corinthians 13:4–5 _____ _____

Humility

   Psalm 131:1–2 _____ _____

Purity

   Matthew 5:27–28 _____ _____

Honesty/Integrity

   Proverbs 28:13 _____ _____

Faith/Trust

   Hebrews 11:1 _____ _____

Good Works

   James 1:27 _____ _____

Use this page to record the verses you would like to memorize in the future that may not fit into the categories already listed.

AN IN-DEPTH
BIBLE STUDY PLAN

IF YOU HAVE THE AMBITION AND DESIRE TO STUDY THE WORD OF GOD in depth, here is a simple plan. You can study one of the verses you have memorized, or a passage consisting of several verses, over a period of seven days.

Day 1
What is the main topic of the verse or the text? Summarize the text in your own words.

Day 2
Read the context (i.e., the verses before and after the text). How does the passage relate to the context? Does the verse summarize the context or clarify it?

Day 3
Read this verse repeatedly and focus on a different word each time. What do these words mean? Use a Bible dictionary if necessary.

Day 4
Look up other cross references or verses in the Bible that can help you understand the text you are studying. How do these other verses help you have a better understanding?

Day 5
What is the intent of this passage? Read commentaries and look at maps. What is the historical background? What was the intent of the writer at that time? What was the intent of the Holy Spirit, the Author, for people then?

Day 6

What is the intent of the Holy Spirit, the Author of the Bible, for your life today? What applications can you make to your life?

- Is there a command you should obey?
- Is there a promise you can claim?
- Is there a sin you should confess or avoid?
- Is there an example you can follow?
- What are the practical steps you need to take?

Day 7

Review what you have written in the past six days. Organize what you have learned in the form of an outline. Given the opportunity in a small group or with a friend, you can share your discoveries about this text in a brief, organized manner.

"Do not let this Book of the Law depart from your mouth; meditate on it day and night, so that you may be careful to do everything written in it. Then you will be prosperous and successful" (Joshua 1:8).

BIBLE READING
HIGHLIGHTS RECORD

Photocopy the weeklong highlights record, or record your thoughts in a quiet-time notebook.

Translation: _____   Year: _____

Sunday   Date: _____   All I read today: _____

Best thing I marked today (reference): _____

Thought: _____

_____

_____

_____

_____

How it impressed me: _____

_____

_____

_____

_____

_____

_____

_____

_____

_____

_____

_____

_____

Monday   Date: All I read today:

Best thing I marked today (reference):

Thought:

How it impressed me:

Tuesday   Date: All I read today:

Best thing I marked today (reference):

Thought:

How it impressed me:

Wednesday Date: _____ All I read today: _____

Best thing I marked today (reference): _____

Thought: _____

_____

_____

_____

_____

How it impressed me: _____

_____

_____

_____

_____

_____

_____

_____

Thursday Date: _____ All I read today: _____

Best thing I marked today (reference): _____

Thought: _____

_____

_____

_____

How it impressed me: _____

_____

_____

_____

_____

_____

_____

Friday
Date: All I read today: _____

Best thing I marked today (reference): _____

Thought: _____

_____

_____

_____

_____

How it impressed me: _____

_____

_____

_____

_____

_____

_____

_____

Saturday
Date: All I read today: _____

Best thing I marked today (reference): _____

Thought: _____

_____

_____

_____

How it impressed me: _____

_____

_____

_____

_____

_____

_____

_____

CHRONOLOGICAL

BIBLE READING PLAN

This is one of many plans to help you read the Bible in the order it is believed to be originally written. You may want to photocopy this plan and use it as a bookmark in your Bible.

JANUARY

1 Genesis 1–3

2 Genesis 4–7

3 Genesis 8–11

4 Job 1–4

5 Job 5–9

6 Job 10–14

7 Job 15–19

8 Job 20–24

9 Job 25–30

10 Job 31–34

11 Job 35–38

12 Job 39–42; Genesis 12

13 Genesis 13–16

14 Genesis 17–19

15 Genesis 20–22

16 Genesis 23–24

17 Genesis 25–27:29

18 Genesis 27:30–29

19 Genesis 30–31

20 Genesis 32–34

21 Genesis 35–37

22 Genesis 38–40

23 Genesis 41–42

24 Genesis 43–44

25 Genesis 45–47

26 Genesis 48–50

27 Exodus 1–3

28 Exodus 4–6

29 Exodus 7–9:21

30 Exodus 9:22–12:16

31 Exodus 12:17–14

FEBRUARY

1 Exodus 15–17

2 Exodus 18–20

3 Exodus 21–22

4 Exodus 23–25

5 Exodus 26–28

6 Exodus 29–30

7 Exodus 31–33

8 Exodus 34–36:19

9 Exodus 36:20–38

10 Exodus 39–40; Leviticus 1

11 Leviticus 2–4

12 Leviticus 5–7

13 Leviticus 8–10

14 Leviticus 11–13:37

15 Leviticus 13:38–14

16 Leviticus 15–16

17 Leviticus 17–19

18 Leviticus 20–22

19 Leviticus 23–25:17

20 Leviticus 25:18–26

21 Leviticus 27; Numbers 1

22 Numbers 2–3

23 Numbers 4–5

24 Numbers 6–7:77

25 Numbers 7:78–10

26 Numbers 11–13

27 Numbers 14–15

28 Numbers 16–18:13

MARCH

1 Numbers 18:14–20

2 Numbers 21–22

3 Numbers 23–26:27

4 Numbers 26:28–28

5 Numbers 29–31

6 Numbers 32–34

7 Numbers 35–36; Deuteronomy 1

8 Deuteronomy 2–3

9 Deuteronomy 4–5

10 Deuteronomy 6–8

11 Deuteronomy 9–11

12 Deuteronomy 12–14

13 Deuteronomy 15–17

14 Deuteronomy 18–20

15 Deuteronomy 21–23

16 Deuteronomy 24–26

17 Deuteronomy 27–28

18 Deuteronomy 29–31

19 Deuteronomy 32–33

20 Deuteronomy 34; Psalm 90; Joshua 1–2

21 Joshua 3–5

22 Joshua 6–7

23 Joshua 8–9

24 Joshua 10–12

25 Joshua 13–15

26 Joshua 16–19

27 Joshua 20–22

28 Joshua 23–24; Judges 1

29 Judges 2–4

30 Judges 5–6

31 Judges 7–8

A P R I L

1 Judges 9; Ruth 1

2 Ruth 2–4

3 Judges 10–12

4 Judges 13–15

5 Judges 16–18

6 Judges 19–20

7 Judges 21; 1 Samuel 1–2:17

8 1 Samuel 2:18–5

9 1 Samuel 6–9:14

10 1 Samuel 9:15–12

11 1 Samuel 13–14

12 1 Samuel 15–16; Psalm 8, 23

13 1 Samuel 17–18; Psalm 11

14 1 Samuel 19; Psalm 58–59

15 1 Samuel 20–21; Psalm 34, 56

16 1 Samuel 22; Psalm 7, 52, 57, 63–64

17 Psalm 109, 140–141; 1 Samuel 23; Psalm 12–13

18 Psalm 14, 17, 22, 31, 36, 54

19 1 Samuel 24; Psalm 35, 142

20 1 Samuel 25–26; Psalm 16, 70; 1 Samuel 27; Psalm 86

21 1 Samuel 28–31

22 2 Samuel 1–3

23 2 Samuel 4–5; Psalm 15, 24, 29–30, 101, 133, 144

24 2 Samuel 6; Psalm 110; 2 Samuel 7; Psalm 2, 5

25 Psalm 19, 103, 105, 122, 131; 2 Samuel 8

26 Psalm 9–10, 18, 25

27 Psalm 26, 60, 108, 124; 2 Samuel 9–10; Psalm 53

28 2 Samuel 11–12; Psalm 6, 20

29 Psalm 21, 32, 38–40, 51

30 2 Samuel 13–14

M A Y

1 2 Samuel 15–16

2 2 Samuel 17 Psalm 3–4, 27–28, 41

3 Psalm 55, 61–62, 69, 143

4 2 Samuel 18–19

5 2 Samuel 20–21; Psalm 65

6 2 Samuel 22; Psalm 37, 68

7 Psalm 138–139; 145; 2 Samuel 23

8 2 Samuel 24; 1 Kings 1

9 1 Kings 2–3

10 1 Kings 4; Proverbs 1–3

11 Proverbs 4–8

12 Proverbs 9–13

13 Proverbs 14–17

14 Proverbs 18–21

15 Proverbs 22–25

16 Proverbs 26–29

17 Proverbs 30–31 Song of Solomon 1–3

18 Song of Solomon 4–8; 1 Kings 5

19 1 Kings 6–7

20 1 Kings 8

21 1 Kings 9–10; Psalm 72, 127

22 1 Kings 11; Ecclesiastes 1–2

23 Ecclesiastes 3–7

24 Ecclesiastes 8–12

25 1 Kings 12–13

26 1 Kings 14–16:10

27 1 Kings 16:11–18:40

28 1 Kings 18:41–20

29 1 Kings 21–22

30 2 Kings 1–3

31 2 Kings 4–5

J U N E

1 2 Kings 6–7

2 2 Kings 8–9

3 2 Kings 10–11

4 Obadiah; 2 Kings 12–13

5 2 Kings 14; Jonah

6 Amos 1–5

7 Amos 6–9; 2 Kings 15:1–15

8 2 Kings 15:16–38; Hosea 1–4

9 Hosea 5–9

10 Hosea 10–14

11 2 Kings 16–17

12 2 Kings 18–19

13 2 Kings 20–21; Nahum 1–2

14 Nahum 3; 2 Kings 22–23

15 2 Kings 24–25; 1 Chronicles 1

16 1 Chronicles 2–4

17 1 Chronicles 5–6

18 1 Chronicles 7–9

19 1 Chronicles 10–12

20 1 Chronicles 13–16

21 Psalm 95–100, 106

22 Psalm 107, 118, 125; 1 Chronicles 17

23 Psalm 1, 89, 111–112, 146; 1 Chronicles 18

24 Psalm 33, 121, 129; 1 Chronicles 19–21

25 Psalm 123, 130; 1 Chronicles 22; Psalm 119:1–80

26 Psalm 119:81–176; 1 Chronicles 23

27 1 Chronicles 24–25; Psalm 50, 73–74

28 Psalm 75–78

29 Psalm 79–83, 150; 1 Chronicles 26

30 1 Chronicles 27–28; Psalm 91

JULY

1 1 Chronicles 29; Psalm 71; 2 Chronicles 1

2 2 Chronicles 2–5

3 2 Chronicles 6–7

4 Psalm 42–49

5 Psalm 66–67, 84–85, 87–88, 92–94, 117, 128

6 Psalm 132, 134–136, 148; 2 Chronicles 8–9:12

7 2 Chronicles 9:13–31; Psalm 104, 114; 2 Chronicles 10–11

8 2 Chronicles 12–15

9 2 Chronicles 16–19

10 2 Chronicles 20–22

11 2 Chronicles 23; Joel 1–2

12 Joel 3; 2 Chronicles 24–25

13 2 Chronicles 26–27; Isaiah 1–2

14 Isaiah 3–6

15 2 Chronicles 28; Isaiah 7–8

16 Isaiah 9–12

17 2 Chronicles 29; Psalm 102, 115

18 2 Chronicles 30–31; Isaiah 13

19 Isaiah 14–18

20 Isaiah 19–22

21 Isaiah 23–27

22 Isaiah 28–30

23 Isaiah 31–35

24 Isaiah 36–37

25 Isaiah 38–39; Micah 1–4

26 Micah 5–7; 2 Chronicles 32

27 Isaiah 40–42

28 Isaiah 43–44

29 Isaiah 45–48

30 Isaiah 49–51

31 Isaiah 52–56

AUGUST

1 Isaiah 57–60

2 Isaiah 61–65

3 Isaiah 66; 2 Chronicles 33–34:7

4 Zephaniah

5 2 Chronicles 34:8–35

6 Jeremiah 1–3

7 Jeremiah 4–6

8 Jeremiah 7–9

9 Jeremiah 10–12

10 Jeremiah 13–15

11 Jeremiah 16–18

12 Jeremiah 19–20; 2 Chronicles 36:1–4; Jeremiah 26

13 Jeremiah 25, 35

14 Jeremiah 36, 45–47

15 Jeremiah 48–49

16 Habakkuk; Daniel 1

17 Daniel 2–3

18 Daniel 4; 2 Chronicles 36:5–10; Jeremiah 24, 27

19 Jeremiah 28–30

20 Jeremiah 31; Ezekiel 1

21 Ezekiel 2–5

22 Ezekiel 6–9

23 Ezekiel 10–12

24 Ezekiel 13–16:19

25 Ezekiel 16:20–17

26 Ezekiel 18–20:29

27 Ezekiel 20:30–22

28 Ezekiel 23–24

29 Ezekiel 25; Jeremiah 21–22

30 Jeremiah 23, 32

31 Jeremiah 33–34; Ezekiel 29

SEPTEMBER

1 Ezekiel 30, 26

2 Ezekiel 27–28, 31

3 Jeremiah 37–39

4 Jeremiah 52:1–30; 40:1–6; 2 Chronicles 36:11–21; Jeremiah 40:7–41

5 Jeremiah 42–44

6 Jeremiah 50–51:23

7 Jeremiah 51:24–64; Lamentations 1

8 Lamentations 2–4

9 Lamentations 5; Psalm 137; Ezekiel 32; 33:1–16

10 Ezekiel 33:17–36:15

11 Ezekiel 36:16–38

12 Ezekiel 39–40

13 Ezekiel 41–43

14 Ezekiel 44–45

15 Ezekiel 46–47

16 Ezekiel 48; Jeremiah 52:31–34; Daniel 7

17 Daniel 8, 5

18 Daniel 6, 9; 2 Chronicles 36:22–23

19 Daniel 10–11

20 Daniel 12; Ezra 1–2; Psalm 126; Ezra 3

21 Ezra 4; Haggai; Zechariah 1

22 Zechariah 2–7

23 Zechariah 8–12

24 Zechariah 13–14; Ezra 5–6

25 Psalm 116; Esther 1–3

26 Esther 4–8

27 Esther 9–10; Ezra 7

28 Ezra 8–10

29 Nehemiah 1–3

30 Nehemiah 4–6; Psalm 113, 120

O C T O B E R

1 Psalm 147, 149; Nehemiah 7–8

2 Nehemiah 9–10

3 Nehemiah 11 – 12:43; Malachi 1

4 Malachi 2–4; Nehemiah 12:44–13

5 Matthew 1–4

6 Matthew 5–6

7 Matthew 7–9

8 Matthew 10–12:21

9 Matthew 12:22–13

10 Matthew 14–16

11 Matthew 17–19

12 Matthew 20–21

13 Matthew 22–23

14 Matthew 24–25

15 Matthew 26

16 Matthew 27–28

17 Mark 1–3

18 Mark 4–6:29

19 Mark 6:30–8

20 Mark 9–10

21 Mark 11–12

22 Mark 13–14

23 Mark 15–16; Luke 1:1–38

24 Luke 1:39–3:18

25 Luke 3:19–5

26 Luke 6–7

27 Luke 8–9:45

28 Luke 9:46–11:28

29 Luke 11:29–12

30 Luke 13–15

31 Luke 16–18

N O V E M B E R

1 Luke 19–20

2 Luke 21–22

3 Luke 23–24

4 Acts 1–2

5 Acts 3–5

6 Acts 6–7

7 Acts 8–9

8 Acts 10–12

9 James 1–4

10 James 5; Acts 13–14

11 Acts 15–16

12 Acts 17–18:11; 1 Thessalonians 1–2

13 1 Thessalonians 3–5; 2 Thessalonians 1–2

14 2 Thessalonians 3; Acts 18:12–19:20; Galatians 1–2

15 Galatians 3–6

16 Acts 19:21–22; 1 Corinthians 1–4

17 1 Corinthians 5–8

18 1 Corinthians 9–11

19 1 Corinthians 12–14

20 1 Corinthians 15–16; Acts 19:23–41

21 Acts 20:1; 2 Corinthians 1–4

22 2 Corinthians 5–8

23 2 Corinthians 9–11

24 2 Corinthians 12–13; Acts 20:2–3a; Romans 1

25 Romans 2–4

26 Romans 5–7

27 Romans 8–10

28 Romans 11–14

29 Romans 15–16; Acts 20:3b–38

30 Acts 21–22

D E C E M B E R

1 Acts 23–25

2 Acts 26–27

3 Acts 28; Ephesians 1–3

4 Ephesians 4–6; Colossians 1

5 Colossians 2–4; Philemon

6 Philippians

7 Jude; 1 Timothy 1–4

8 1 Timothy 5–6; Titus

9 2 Timothy

10 1 Peter 1–4

11 1 Peter 5; 2 Peter

12 Hebrews 1–6

13 Hebrews 7–9

14 Hebrews 10–11

15 Hebrews 12–13; John 1

16 John 2–4

17 John 5–6

18 John 7–8

19 John 9–10

20 John 11–12

21 John 13–14

22 John 15–17

23 John 18–19

24 John 20–21; 1 John 1–2

25 1 John 3–5; 2 John

26 3 John; Revelation 1–2

27 Revelation 3–6

28 Revelation 7–11

29 Revelation 12–15

30 Revelation 16–19

31 Revelation 20–22

APPENDIX 6

TRUST LIST

MEDITATING AND PRAYING OVER A TRUST LIST IS AN EXERCISE THAT IS
very pleasing to God. At times we focus on pleasing Him when we should
focus on trusting Him. When we *trust God*, we end up *pleasing Him*.

Make up your list and come back to it for rejuvenation and renewal.
Start every statement with the phrase "I trust You that. . . " Here are
some trust prayers from my list.

1. I trust You that I am free from any and all condemnation. *"Therefore, there is now no condemnation for those who are in Christ Jesus"*
(Romans 8:1).

2. I trust You that You have already blessed me with every spiritual
blessing. *"Praise be to the God and Father of our Lord Jesus Christ,
who has blessed us in the heavenly realms with every spiritual blessing in Christ"* (Ephesians 1:3). Open my eyes to see how You have
already blessed me.

3. I trust You, Father, that I am totally accepted by You because
You see me through the lenses of what Jesus did on the cross and
through the resurrection. I am fully pleasing to You. When You
look at me, I am wrapped from my head to my feet with the robe
of Christ's righteousness. *"I delight greatly in the LORD; my soul
rejoices in my God. For he has clothed me with garments of salvation
and arrayed me in a robe of righteousness"* (Isaiah 61:10).

4. I trust You, Father, that You can help me have the right attitude
toward my circumstances and give You thanks. *"Give thanks in all
circumstances, for this is God's will for you in Christ Jesus"* (1 Thessalonians 5:18). *"I heard and my heart pounded, my lips quivered
at the sound; decay crept into my bones, and my legs trembled. Yet*

I will wait patiently for the day of calamity to come on the nation invading us. Though the fig tree does not bud and there are no grapes on the vines, though the olive crop fails and the fields produce no food, though there are no sheep in the pen and no cattle in the stalls, yet I will rejoice in the LORD; I will be joyful in God my Savior. The Sovereign LORD is my strength; he makes my feet like the feet of a deer, he enables me to go on the heights" (Habakkuk 3:16–19).

5. I trust You, Lord, that You are leading me on a road of maturity on which I am learning to cope with my circumstances. *"Consider it pure joy, my brothers, whenever you face trials of many kinds, because you know that the testing of your faith develops perseverance. Perseverance must finish its work so that you may be mature and complete, not lacking anything"* (James 1:2–4).

6. I trust You, Father, that Jesus Christ today went ahead of me and paved the way as my *Pioneer.* I trust You, Father, that Jesus is going to come right behind me today to sustain me and heal me as my *Perfecter.* *"Let us fix our eyes on Jesus, the author and perfecter of our faith, who for the joy set before him endured the cross, scorning its shame, and sat down at the right hand of the throne of God"* (Hebrews 12:2).

7. I trust your promise, Jesus, that You are inviting me today and every day to carry with You Your yoke and experience genuine rest. *"'Come to me, all who are weary and burdened, and I will give you rest. Take my yoke upon you and learn from me, for I am gentle and humble in heart, and you will find rest for your souls. For my yoke is easy and my burden is light'"* (Matthew 11:28–30).

8. I trust You, Father, that You are able to keep me from falling. *"To him who is able to keep you from falling and to present you before his glorious presence without fault and with great joy—to the only God our Savior be glory, majesty, power and authority, through Jesus Christ our Lord, before all ages, now and forevermore! Amen"* (Jude 1:24–25).

9. I trust You, Father, that I am free from the burden of the law. What really matters is that Christ lives in me. *"I tried keeping rules and working my head off to please God, and it didn't work. So I quit being a 'law man' so that I could be God's man. Christ's life showed*

me how, and enabled me to do it. I identified myself completely with him. Indeed, I have been crucified with Christ. My ego is no longer central. It is no longer important that I appear righteous before you or have your good opinion, and I am no longer driven to impress God. Christ lives in me. The life you see me living is not 'mine,' but it is lived by faith in the Son of God, who loved me and gave himself for me. I am not going to go back on that. Is it not clear to you that to go back to that old rule-keeping, peer-pleasing religion would be an abandonment of everything personal and free in my relationship with God? I refuse to do that, to repudiate God's grace. If a living relationship with God could come by rule keeping, then Christ died unnecessarily" (Galatians 2:19–21, *The Message*).

RECOMMENDED BOOKS

All That the Prophets Have Spoken by Yehia Sa'a. This book will give you a good foundation in understanding and getting to know the Bible. Available from GoodSeed International (www.goodseed.com).

The Case for the Resurrection of Jesus by Gary R. Habermas and Michael R. Licona. Available from Kregel Publications.

A Muslim's Heart: What Every Christian Needs to Know to Share Christ with Muslims by Dr. Edward J. Hoskins. Available from Dawson Media, www.dawsonmedia.com or (888) 547-9635.

The Unseen Reality: A Panoramic View of Spiritual Warfare by Nabeel Jabbour. Download at www.nabeeljabbour.com.

Whose Promised Land? The Continuing Crisis over Israel and Palestine by Colin Chapman. Available from Baker Books.